Great Sedo

REVISED SECOND EDITION

AN EASY-TO-USE GUIDE
FOR THE 55 GREATEST HIKING
TRAILS IN SEDONA, ARIZONA

FEATURING OUR
12 FAVORITE HIKES

William Bohan

and

David Butler

Non-liability Statement

The authors have taken every precaution to ensure that the information contained within is up-to-date, accurate and reflects trail conditions when this guide was published. However, trail conditions frequently change because of weather, Forest Service activity or other causes. The GPS data included were obtained from a model 60CSx Garmin GPS unit. Because the data are only as accurate as the sensitivity of the GPS unit, some inaccuracies may be present. Users of GPS data are urged to use common sense when hiking. Always stay on the trail. The authors, publisher, contributors, and all those involved in the preparation of this book, either directly or indirectly, disclaim any liability for injuries, accidents, and damages whatsoever that may occur to those using this guide. You are responsible for your health and safety while hiking the trails.

Front Cover Photo: Devil's Bridge
Back Cover Photo: Brins Mesa Overlook

Table of Contents

About the Authors

This guide is a result of a collaboration between William Bohan and David Butler, two avid Sedona hikers, who have completed over 500 Sedona hikes between them.

William was born in Michigan and was an Executive Engineer with a major auto company until he retired in 2001. He moved to Sedona in 2002 and began hiking shortly thereafter. In 2005, he launched a website (http://greatsedonahikes.com) as a way to easily share hike photos with his fellow hikers. William continues to hike the trails in Sedona and updates the information on his website on a regular basis.

David was born in Ohio and was Associate Dean of the College of the Arts at a major Ohio university until he retired in 2003. After moving to Sedona, he began hiking with a local hiking group. He is an enthusiastic photographer, who has hiked over 100 trails in the area with his wife Ruth.

This second edition guidebook includes the greatest 55 hikes in Sedona, as rated by William and David. They have hiked most of the trails in the Sedona area and each author has a broad-based wealth of hiking experience. There are other trails available in the Sedona area, but the ones included in this book are simply the <u>Great Sedona Hikes</u>.

If you have suggestions or comments on the guidebook, email William and David at: hikebook@greatsedonahikes.com

William Bohan   David Butler

Changes to This Edition

This Second Edition includes all 50 hikes from the First Edition plus 5 additional hikes: Brins Mesa Overlook, Cockscomb/Aerie, HT, Rabbit Ears and Telephone Trail. The Master Hike Locator Map has been improved and all individual hike maps have added detail, including elevation data. Trail descriptions and waypoints have been updated to the latest trail conditions. Our 12 favorite hikes are now highlighted in a special section.

Acknowledgments

The authors would like to acknowledge several individuals for their contributions to this book. They are:
Our wives, Nancy Williams and Ruth Butler for their efforts in editing this work; René and Michele Braun, Lou Camp, Marie Concher, Mary Heyborne, Tom and Peg Likens, Helen Mueller, Roberta Petersen, Tom and Becky Solon, Darryl and Lorna Thompson, Mark Watson, and Charlie and Marilyn Weaver, for their comments and companionship while hiking the trails. We mourn the loss of our friend and hiking companion, Alain Concher.

Hiking Tips

The stunning red rock formations, moderate temperatures and close proximity to the trails make hiking in Sedona an experience unlike anywhere else in the world, but hiking is not without risk.

It is very important to be prepared, even for a day hike. The environment is very dry in Sedona so bring enough water to stay hydrated and drink water throughout the hike. In addition:

- Let someone know where you'll be hiking, hike with at least one other person and complete your hike before sunset
- If you must hike alone, leave a note in your vehicle stating where you intend to hike and when you expect to return
- Check the weather before you begin hiking, and reschedule your hike if inclement weather is predicted
- Wear a hat and sunscreen
- Wear hiking boots or good walking shoes, as the trails can be uneven and rocky
- Carry a first-aid kit, a fully charged cell phone (although many hiking trails do not have cell phone service), flashlight, compass, map, portable GPS unit, rescue whistle, pocketknife and a snack
- Trailhead parking lots can be the target of thieves so don't leave valuables in your vehicle
- Downhill hikers have the right-of-way in most instances because footing is more tenuous downhill than uphill. If hiking uphill, step aside and let downhill hikers pass
- Bicyclists are supposed to yield to all trail users, but use common sense and step aside when appropriate
- Remember, hiking is not a race. Slow down and look around while hiking; many times the best views are behind you

Alphabetical List of Included Hikes

(F) symbol indicates a Favorite Hike

(P) symbol indicates Recreation Pass required or Special Fee area. See page 14 for more information.

Sedona Average Weather
& Sunrise/Sunset Data

	Temperature F		Precipitation (Inches)	Sunrise	Sunset
	Daily High	Daily Low		(1st of Month)	
January	56	30	2.10	7:32 AM	5:30 PM
February	60	33	2.16	7:24 AM	5:58 PM
March	65	37	2.47	6:57 AM	6:24 PM
April	73	42	1.16	6:16 AM	6:48 PM
May	82	49	0.71	5:40 AM	7:10 PM
June	93	58	0.36	5:19 AM	7:32 PM
July	97	64	1.65	5:21 AM	7:42 PM
August	94	63	1.90	5:40 AM	7:29 PM
September	88	58	1.94	6:02 AM	6:55 PM
October	77	48	1.67	6:22 AM	6:14 PM
November	64	36	1.38	6:46 AM	5:37 PM
December	57	31	1.51	7:14 AM	5:20 PM
Average	75	46	1.50		

Vortex Information

If you come to Sedona with the thought of visiting a vortex or two, you are not alone. It's estimated that more than half of Sedona visitors are interested in experiencing the power of vortexes (vortices). There are four main Sedona vortexes: Airport Mesa, Bell Rock, Boynton Canyon, and Cathedral Rock. All four locations are described in this guidebook. We suggest that you approach each vortex without preconceived ideas of what you may experience, and just let the experience "happen." If nothing else, you'll enjoy some of Sedona's finest views. And if you'd like additional information on the four main vortexes, plus information on the location of 10 additional "power spots" where vortex energy has been reported, you might be interested in our *Hiking the Vortexes* publication, available at many Sedona retailers and at https://createspace.com/3538560.

GPS Data

When you read the hike descriptions, you will find numbers in curly brackets such as {1}, {2}, and so on. These numbers refer to the GPS checkpoints in the maps below each of the hike descriptions. In addition, elevation data for each of the GPS coordinates are shown on the maps. Note that the elevation data does not necessarily reflect the maximum or minimum elevations you will experience on the hike. Specific GPS data, including "tracks" in the universal .gpx format for all the hikes contained in this guidebook are available at: http://greatsedonahikes.com.

Master Hike Locator

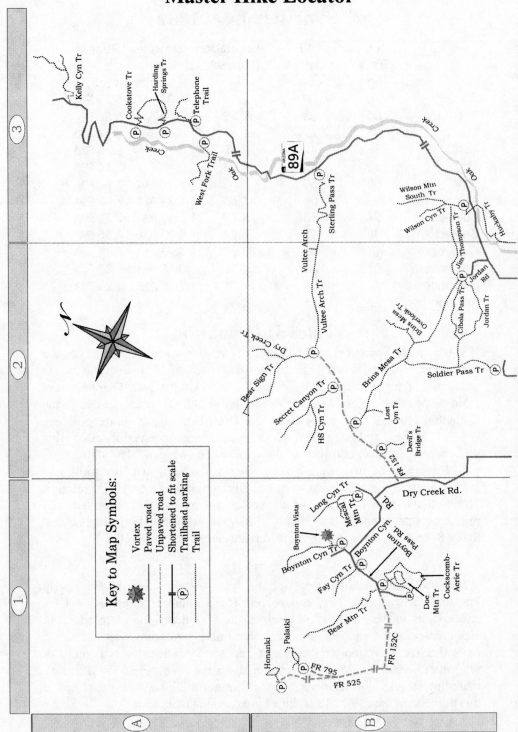

Key to Map Symbols:

Vortex
Paved road
Unpaved road
Shortened to fit scale
Trailhead parking
Trail

Master Hike Locator

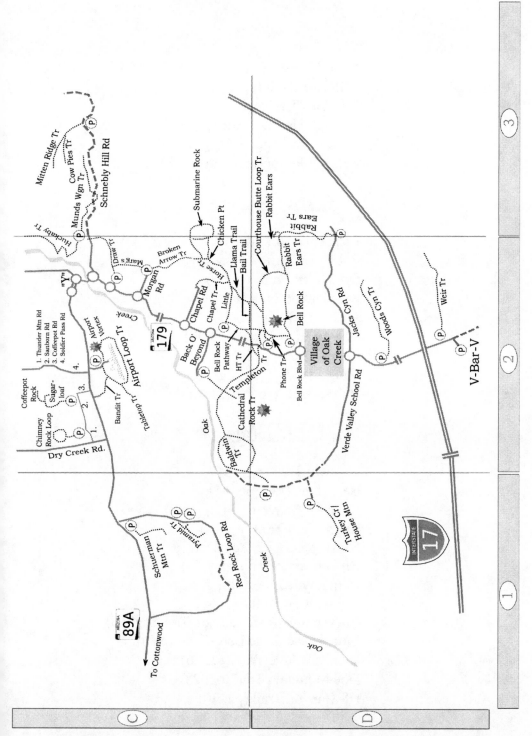

Hikes Rated by Level of Difficulty

Easy

Airport Vortex (pg. 42)
Coffeepot Trail (pg. 58)
Cow Pies Trail (pg. 64)
Honanki Heritage Site (pg. 68)
Palatki Heritage Site (pg. 96)
V-Bar-V Petroglyph Site (pg. 114)

Easy to Moderate

Airport Loop Trail (pg. 40)
Bell Rock Vortex (pg. 46)
Dry Creek Trail (pg. 66)
Fay Canyon Trail (pg. 30)
Jordan Trail (pg. 78)
Kelly Canyon Trail (pg. 80)
Llama Trail (pg. 82)
Marg's Draw Trail (pg. 88)
Vultee Arch Trail (pg. 116)

Moderate

Baldwin Trail (pg. 16)
Bear Sign Trail (pg. 44)
Boynton Canyon Trail (pg. 20)
Brins Mesa Trail (pg. 48)
Brins Mesa Overlook Trail (pg. 22)
Broken Arrow Trail (pg. 24)
Chimney Rock Trail (pg. 52)
Cibola Pass Trail (pg. 54)
Cockscomb to Aerie Loop Trail (pg. 56)
Courthouse Butte Loop Trail (pg. 62)
Devil's Bridge Trail (pg. 26)
Doe Mountain Trail (pg. 28)
HS Canyon Trail (pg. 70)

Hikes Rated by Level of Difficulty

Moderate (cont'd)

Hard

Hikes By Feature

Hikes To/Near Arches
Devil's Bridge Trail (pg. 26)
Fay Canyon Trail (pg. 30)
Soldier Pass Trail (pg. 36)
Vultee Arch Trail (pg. 116)

Indian Ruin Hikes
Boynton Canyon Trail (pg. 20)
Honanki Heritage Site (pg. 68)
Lost Canyon Trail (pg. 86)
Mescal Mountain Trail (pg. 90)
Palatki Heritage Site (pg. 96)
V-Bar-V Petroglyph Site (pg. 114)

Vortex Hikes
Airport Vortex Trail (pg. 42)
Bell Rock Trail (pg. 46)
Boynton Canyon (Vista) Trail (pg. 20)
Cathedral Rock Trail (pg. 50)

Water Hikes
Baldwin Trail (pg. 16)
Huckaby Trail (pg. 74)
Munds Wagon Trail - spring
   runoff only (pg. 94)
Templeton Trail (pg. 110)
Weir Trail (pg. 118)
West Fork Trail (pg. 38)
Woods Canyon Trail – spring runoff only
(pg. 124)

Shaded Trails

The following trails provide partial shade and may be suitable for summer hiking. But be sure to take extra water when hiking in the summer.

Baldwin Trail (on the north and east side) (pg. 16)
Bear Sign Trail (pg. 44)
Boynton Canyon Trail (past Enchantment Resort) (pg. 20)
Cibola Pass Trail (pg. 54)
Cookstove to Harding Springs Trails (pg. 60)
Devil's Bridge Trail (pg. 26)
Dry Creek Trail (pg. 66)
HS Canyon Trail (pg. 70)
HT Trail (pg. 72)
Huckaby Trail (near Oak Creek) (pg. 74)
Jordan Trail (pg. 78)
Kelly Canyon Trail (pg. 80)
Long Canyon Trail (after 1 mile) (pg. 84)
Munds Wagon Trail (pg. 94)
Sterling Pass Trail (pg. 104)
Telephone Trail (pg. 108)
West Fork Trail (pg. 38)

Muddy Trail Conditions

After wet weather, the following trails may be suitable for hiking. Do not hike if thunderstorm, lightning or flash flood warnings are present. Drizzles can quickly turn into electrical storms.

Baldwin Trail (pg. 16)
Boynton Canyon Trail (pg. 20)
Courthouse Butte Loop Trail (pg. 62)
Doe Mountain Trail (pg. 28)
Fay Canyon Trail (pg. 30)
Jim Thompson Trail (pg. 76)
Little Horse Trail (pg. 32)
Llama Trail (pg. 82)
Marg's Draw Trail (pg. 88)
Munds Wagon Trail (pg. 94)
Schuerman Mountain Trail (pg. 102)
Templeton Trail (pg. 110)
Wilson Canyon Trail (pg. 120)

Required Parking Pass

If you park on the Coconino National Forest around Sedona, you may need to display a Recreation Pass. If you park on private property, you do not need to display a Recreation Pass. Nor do you need to display a Pass if you are driving around enjoying the scenery, stopping to take a photo, or parking temporarily and remaining near your vehicle.

A Recreation Pass is required for trailhead parking at many of the trails listed in this guide. [See page 6, Alphabetical List of Included Hikes and look for this symbol **(P)**.] It is also required for the Bootlegger, Banjo Bill, Halfway and Encinoso picnic areas in Oak Creek Canyon. Additionally, there are 3 special fee areas: Crescent Moon Ranch/Red Rock Crossing ($9), West Fork Trail ($9), and Grasshopper Point Picnic Area ($8). Each area charges a separate, unique fee.

A Recreation Pass is any of the following: 1) a National Parks Pass, also known as a Federal Interagency Annual Pass; 2) a Senior Pass, also known as a Federal Interagency Senior Pass, issued to U.S. residents 62 years of age and older; 3) a Federal Interagency Access Pass, issued to individuals with permanent disabilities; or 4) a Red Rock Pass (described below).

If you do not have any of the above Federal Interagency Passes, you may display a Red Rock Pass, available for sale at many Sedona-area businesses, the Red Rock Ranger Station Visitor Center, the Sedona Chamber of Commerce Uptown Visitor Center, and selected trailheads. The Red Rock Pass is available as a $5 Daily Pass, a $15 Weekly Pass, a $20 Annual Pass, or a $40 Grand Annual Pass.

- The $5 Daily Red Rock Pass permits you to park on the National Forest as described above for the day of issue. It expires at midnight. It does not include the additional parking fees at the 3 special fee areas.
- The $15 Weekly Red Rock Pass permits you to park on the National Forest as described above for 7 days. It does not include the additional parking fees at the 3 special fee areas.
- The $20 Annual Red Rock Pass permits you to park on the National Forest as described above for 1 year. It does not include the additional parking fees at the 3 special fee areas.
- The $40 Grand Annual Pass permits you to park on the National Forest as described above and includes the additional parking fees at the 3 special fee areas for 1 year. It is available at the Red Rock Ranger Station and the Chamber's Uptown Visitor Center.

Because the Red Rock Pass Program changes periodically, check http://www.fs.usda.gov/main/coconino/passes-permits/recreation for the latest information. If you are not sure where you'll be hiking, we recommend that you purchase a Red Rock Pass if you don't have a Recreation Pass to display.

Favorite Hikes

Baldwin Trail **(page 16)**	**Bear Mountain** **(page 18)**	**Boynton Canyon** **(page 20)**
Brins Mesa **Overlook (page 22)**	**Broken Arrow** **(page 24)**	**Devil's Bridge** **(page 26)**
Doe Mountain **(page 28)**	**Fay Canyon** **(page 30)**	**Little Horse** **(page 32)**
Secret Canyon **(page 34)**	**Soldier Pass** **(page 36)**	**West Fork** **(page 38)**

Baldwin Trail

Summary: This loop trail at the base of Cathedral Rock offers some excellent views with an optional short side trip to the banks of Oak Creek

Challenge Level: Moderate

Hiking Distance: About a 3.3 mile loop

Trailhead Directions: Named for Andrew Baldwin, one of the individuals who bought Crescent Moon Ranch in 1936, the trailhead is located on the unpaved portion of Verde Valley School Road. From the "Y" roundabout (the intersection of State Route 89A and State Route 179), drive south on SR 179 about 7 miles to the Jack's Canyon and Verde Valley School Road roundabout then turn right (west). Drive approximately 4.5 miles west on Verde Valley School Road to the parking area on the left (west) side of the road {1}. The trailhead is across the road from the north end of the parking area. There are toilets at the parking area.

Description: The Baldwin Trail, which circles an unnamed red rock butte beside Cathedral Rock, provides excellent panoramic views of Cathedral Rock. After crossing the road, you'll come to a signboard {2}.

16

You can hike the Baldwin Trail in either direction. If you hike in the clockwise direction, you'll intersect an unmarked "social trail" in 0.3 mile {3} and the Templeton Trail after 0.5 mile {4}. Take a side trip by hiking east on the Templeton Trail until it goes beside Oak Creek. After 0.2 mile, look across Oak Creek to see "Buddha Beach," where visitors use river rock to build amazing stacked structures {5}. Periodically, floods knock the structures down, but they are usually quickly replaced. You may be lucky and see hundreds of "buddhas." If you continue east on the Templeton Trail for 0.8 mile, you'll intersect the Cathedral Rock Trail.

Return to the Baldwin Trail then continue around the tall red rock butte. You'll pass some excellent places to stop and enjoy the views {6}{7} on your loop. On your way back you'll intersect an unmarked "social trail" that leads to Verde Valley School Road {8}. For the best photos of Cathedral Rock, do this hike later in the day.

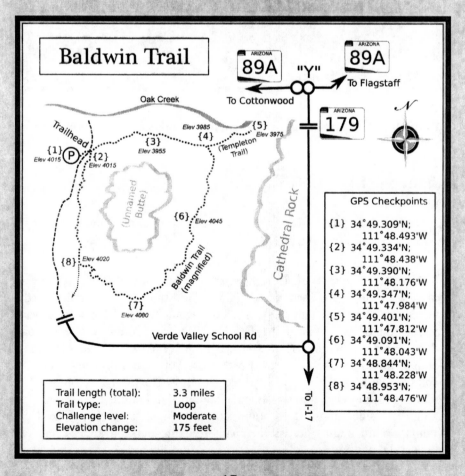

Baldwin Trail

ARIZONA **89A**   "Y"   ARIZONA **89A**   To Flagstaff

To Cottonwood   ARIZONA **179**

N

Oak Creek

Trailhead

Elev 3985   {5}
{4}   Elev 3975
{3}   (Templeton Trail)
Elev 3955

{1}   (P)   {2}
Elev 4015   Elev 4015

(Unnamed Butte)

{6}   Elev 4045

{8}   Elev 4020

Baldwin Trail (magnified)

{7}
Elev 4080

Cathedral Rock

Verde Valley School Rd

To I-17

GPS Checkpoints	
{1}	34°49.309'N; 111°48.493'W
{2}	34°49.334'N; 111°48.438'W
{3}	34°49.390'N; 111°48.176'W
{4}	34°49.347'N; 111°47.984'W
{5}	34°49.401'N; 111°47.812'W
{6}	34°49.091'N; 111°48.043'W
{7}	34°48.844'N; 111°48.228'W
{8}	34°48.953'N; 111°48.476'W

Trail length (total):	3.3 miles
Trail type:	Loop
Challenge level:	Moderate
Elevation change:	175 feet

Bear Mountain Trail

Summary: A strenuous, sunny, in-and-out hike with excellent red rock views

Challenge Level: Hard

Hiking Distance: To the top of Bear Mountain is about 2.5 miles each way; 5 miles round trip

Trailhead Directions: The parking for Bear Mountain hike is shared with the Doe Mountain trail. From the "Y" roundabout (the intersection of State Route 89A and State Route 179), drive west toward Cottonwood on SR 89A about 3 miles. Turn right on Dry Creek Road (where speed limits are strictly enforced). Stay on Dry Creek to a stop sign (about 3 miles) then turn left on Boynton Canyon Road. Proceed about 1.7 miles to a stop sign. Turn left and continue on Boynton Pass Road. The trailhead parking is shared with Doe Mountain Trail and is the second area on the left side, about 1.75 miles from the stop sign {1}. The Bear Mountain Trail begins across the road from the parking area. There are toilets at the parking area.

Description: Bear Mountain provides fantastic views of Doe Mountain (and beyond), and nearby canyons. Climbing from about 4600 feet at the parking lot, you first cross a series of deep washes. You then begin the climb up the mountain. There is a natural stopping place and photo opportunity at elevation 5500 feet {2}. The total elevation gain to the top is some 2000 feet. From the top of Bear Mountain {3}, you can see the San Francisco Peaks in Flagstaff. Note: there are some exposed and extreme drop-offs on parts of this trail – watch your footing.

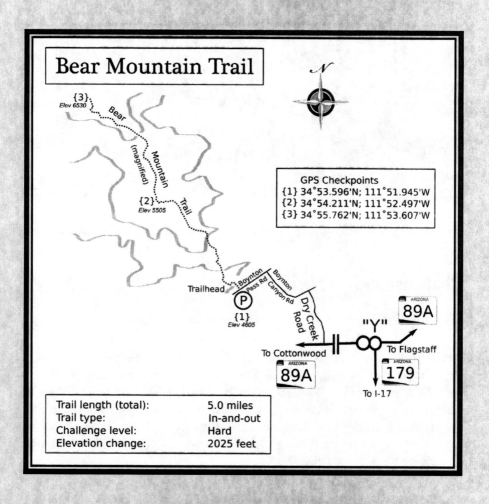

Trail length (total):	5.0 miles
Trail type:	In-and-out
Challenge level:	Hard
Elevation change:	2025 feet

GPS Checkpoints
{1} 34°53.596'N; 111°51.945'W
{2} 34°54.211'N; 111°52.497'W
{3} 34°55.762'N; 111°53.607'W

Boynton Canyon Trail

Summary: An in-and-out hike of a forested canyon with nice red rock views

Challenge Level: Moderate

Hiking Distance: About 3 miles each way; 6 miles round trip

Trailhead Directions: From the "Y" roundabout (the intersection of State Route 89A and State Route 179), drive west toward Cottonwood on SR 89A about 3 miles. Turn right on Dry Creek Road (where speed limits are strictly enforced). Stay on Dry Creek Road to a stop sign (about 3 miles) then turn left on Boynton Canyon Road. Proceed about 1.7 miles to a stop sign. Turn right, the trailhead parking is about 0.1 mile on the right {1}. There are toilets at the parking area.

Description: Boynton Canyon was named for John Boeington, who was a horse rancher in the canyon around 1886. Boynton Canyon is a very popular hike. The nicest part of the hike is located beyond the Enchantment

Resort. We like it for its summer shade and good red rock views. It is also a well-known vortex site. After hiking about 0.25 mile from the parking lot, you'll see a sign for the Boynton Vista Trail to the right {2}. Hike the Vista trail for about 0.4 mile slightly uphill to two tall rock formations, both of which are considered vortex points {3}. After visiting the vortex, return to the Boynton Canyon Trail then continue to the north. The trail beside the Enchantment Resort is rocky and narrow, and is the most difficult part of the trail. Once you are past the Enchantment Resort, the trail follows the canyon floor and widens. After about 1 mile you can see evidence of prior habitation on the right {4}. Soon you'll enter a forest where the trail and views are excellent. You'll see some nice fall colors usually during the third week of October about 2 miles from the trailhead. The trail ends in a box canyon at the base of Secret Mountain {5}.

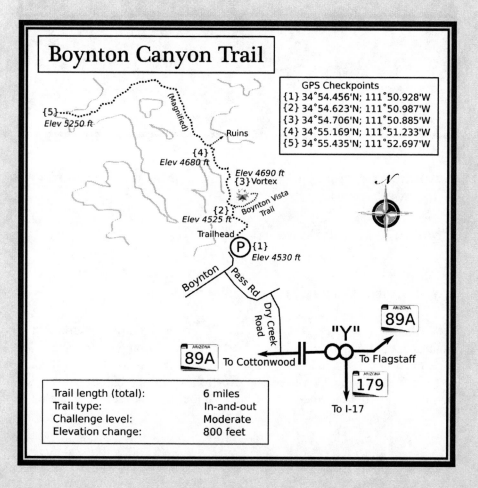

Boynton Canyon Trail

GPS Checkpoints
{1} 34°54.456'N; 111°50.928'W
{2} 34°54.623'N; 111°50.987'W
{3} 34°54.706'N; 111°50.885'W
{4} 34°55.169'N; 111°51.233'W
{5} 34°55.435'N; 111°52.697'W

{5} Elev 5250 ft
(Magnified)
Ruins
{4} Elev 4680 ft
Elev 4690 ft
{3} Vortex
Boynton Vista Trail
{2} Elev 4525 ft
Trailhead
P {1} Elev 4530 ft
Boynton Pass Rd
Dry Creek Road
ARIZONA 89A
"Y"
ARIZONA 89A To Cottonwood
To Flagstaff
ARIZONA 179
To I-17

Trail length (total):	6 miles
Trail type:	In-and-out
Challenge level:	Moderate
Elevation change:	800 feet

Brins Mesa Overlook Trail

Summary: A hike up to a beautiful mesa, then on to a knoll with red rock views all around

Challenge Level: Moderate

Hiking Distance: About 1.5 miles to the edge of Brins Mesa, then another 0.7 mile to the overlook; 4.4 miles round trip

Trailhead Directions: From the "Y" roundabout (the intersection of State Route 89A and State Route 179), drive north on SR 89A about 0.3 mile to Jordan Road. Turn left on Jordan Road then drive to the end. Turn left on Park Ridge Drive then proceed through the paved cul-de-sac, continuing on the dirt road for 0.5 mile to the parking area {1}. There are toilets at the parking area.

Description: The trail begins on the west side of the parking area and as you begin the hike up to Brins Mesa, you are rewarded with some outstanding views. You'll be hiking up about 550 feet to the edge of the mesa. The trail becomes much steeper as you approach it. Immediately after you reach the mesa {2}, look for a faint trail to your right. You'll follow this trail for 0.2 mile and bear left at a fork in the trail {3}. If you go right, you'll shortly come to a scenic outcropping of red rock, which has a nice view {4}. As you continue along the left fork, the trail narrows and follows the north side of Brins Mesa. You'll soon see the Overlook ahead. A moderate amount of scrambling is needed to reach the top of the knoll, but the climb is well worth the effort. At this point you have hiked up another 375 feet from the edge of Brins Mesa. Once on top, there is a spectacular view overlooking Mormon Canyon {5}. Look high up on the rock face to the southeast. If you are lucky, that's where you may see Angel Falls flowing with the spring snow melt.

Brins Mesa Overlook Trail

N

Elev 5455 ft
{5}

GPS Checkpoints
{1} 34°53.287'N; 111°46.098'W
{2} 34°54.021'N; 111°46.765'W
{3} 34°54.157'N; 111°47.567'W
{4} 34°54.147'N; 111°46.542'W
{5} 34°54.507'N; 111°46.374'W

{3}   Elev 5170 ft
Elev 5155 ft   {4}

Brins Mesa Tr

{2}
Elev 5085 ft

(Magnified)

1. Jordan Rd
2. Park Ridge Rd
3. (Unpaved Rd)

P{1}
Trailhead
3. 2.
"Y"   1.
ARIZONA **89A**

To Flagstaff

{1} P
Elev 4520 ft

ARIZONA **179**

To I-17

Trail length (total):	4.4 miles
Trail type:	In-and-out
Challenge level:	Moderate
Elevation change:	935 feet

Broken Arrow Trail

Summary: A sunny, in-and-out trip to Devil's Dining Room, Submarine Rock and Chicken Point with great red rock views

Challenge Level: Moderate

Hiking Distance: About 1.5 miles to Submarine Rock; add 1.2 miles if you take the jeep road to Chicken Point; then 1.7 miles back to the parking area for a total of 4.5 miles round trip

Trailhead Directions: From the "Y" roundabout (the intersection of State Route 89A and State Route 179), drive south on SR 179 1.5 miles to the roundabout at Morgan Road. Turn left (east) on Morgan Road then drive about 0.6 mile to the trailhead parking on your left {1}.

Description: The trail is named for the movie, *Broken Arrow,* which was filmed in the area in 1950. From the parking area, go south across the jeep road to the trail. Initially, the trail essentially parallels the jeep road. After hiking about 0.5 mile, watch for a fence on the left which surrounds a sinkhole known as the Devil's Dining Room {2}. As you continue along the trail, after about 1 mile you'll come to a fork in the trail {3}. Go left to Submarine Rock. The trail has partial shade here. While both ends can be climbed, the north "tower" is a bit steep so go around Submarine Rock on the east side to the south end for an easier climb up and nice views from on top {4}. From here you have two options if you want to go on to Chicken Point, named for thrill-seeking jeep drivers who once dared to drive close to the edge of the point (jeep access is no longer permitted on Chicken Point). The first option is to follow the jeep road. As you look down from the south end of Submarine Rock, you'll see where the Pink Jeeps park. Go down to that parking area and follow the jeep road southwest to get to Chicken Point. Be sure to stay out of the way of the jeeps as you hike along this narrow road. There are areas where the shoulders are high so you do not want to be in the road when a jeep drives by.

The second option to get to Chicken Point is to retrace your steps to the fork in the trail {3} then turn left (south). From Chicken Point the panoramic red rock views are wonderful {5}.

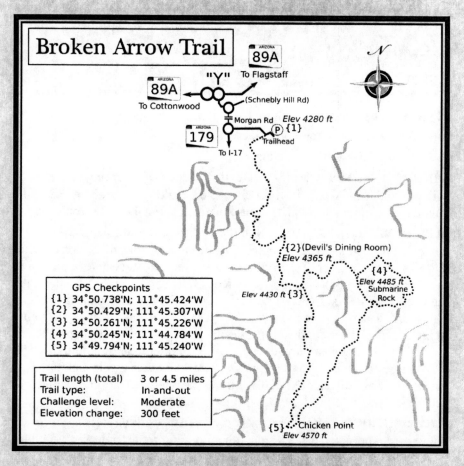

Broken Arrow Trail

GPS Checkpoints
{1} 34°50.738'N; 111°45.424'W
{2} 34°50.429'N; 111°45.307'W
{3} 34°50.261'N; 111°45.226'W
{4} 34°50.245'N; 111°44.784'W
{5} 34°49.794'N; 111°45.240'W

Trail length (total)	3 or 4.5 miles
Trail type:	In-and-out
Challenge level:	Moderate
Elevation change:	300 feet

Devil's Bridge Trail

Summary: A moderate in-and-out climb with steep "stairs" up to the largest natural stone arch in the Sedona area

Challenge Level: Moderate

Hiking Distance: From the Devil's Bridge (DB) parking area about 2 miles round trip: from the FR 152 paved parking area about 6.2 miles round trip: from the Mescal Trail parking area about 4.4 miles round trip

Trailhead Directions: From the "Y" roundabout (the intersection of State Route 89A and State Route 179), drive west toward Cottonwood on SR 89A about 3 miles. Turn right on Dry Creek Road (where speed limits are strictly enforced). Stay on Dry Creek Road for about 2 miles then turn right on Forest Road (FR) 152. Drive for 0.2 mile and park at the Dry Creek Vista parking area on the left {1}. If you have a high clearance vehicle, proceed for another 1.1 miles on the unpaved, very rough FR 152 to the DB parking area on your right {2}. Or rather than turn on to FR 152, a third alternative is to continue on Dry Creek another 1 mile and turn right on Long Canyon Road. Drive 0.3 mile to the Mescal Trail parking area on the right {3}.

Description: From the Dry Creek Vista parking area, go to the signboard where you'll see a small sign pointing to the right for the Chuck Wagon (CW) Trail. As you hike CW, you'll pass the intersection of the

26

trail to the Mescal Trail parking area {3} after 1.1 miles {4}. Continue on the CW Trail for a total of 2.1 miles and turn right on the connector trail to the DB parking area across FR 152 {5}. From the Mescal Trail parking area {3}, hike the connector trail from the east end of the parking area for 0.2 mile and turn left on the CW Trail {4}. Hike for 1 mile to the turn to DB {5}.

Devil's Bridge is a large natural stone arch that you can easily walk on. It is reachable with a moderate amount of climbing (up some 400 feet); the view of the arch and from the arch are well worth the climb. The trail splits about 0.75 mile from the start, 15 feet past where you'll come to a large rock next to the trail {6}. Go straight then right to reach the top of the arch; take the left fork to go beneath the arch. If you take the trail to the top of the arch {7}, you'll be hiking up steep natural stone steps (with no hand rails) so, if you have a fear of heights, you may want to be extra careful on this hike, or only take the left trail to view the arch from beneath.

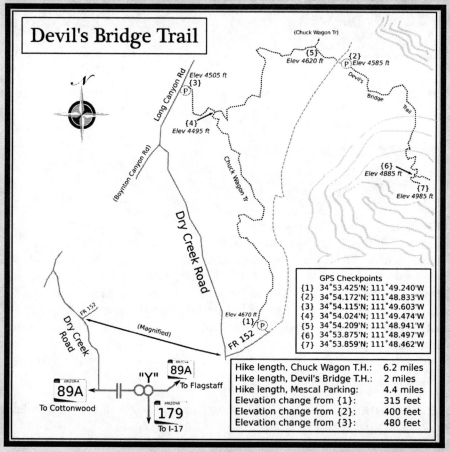

27

Doe Mountain Trail

Summary: The trail climbs up and loops around the top of Doe Mountain, a true, flat-top mesa with panoramic red rock views

Challenge Level: Moderate

Hiking Distance: About 2.6 miles round trip

Trailhead Directions: The parking for Doe Mountain Trail is shared with the Bear Mountain Trail. From the "Y" roundabout (the intersection of State Route 89A and State Route 179), drive west toward Cottonwood on SR 89A about 3 miles. Turn right on Dry Creek Road (where speed limits are strictly enforced). Stay on Dry Creek Road to a stop sign (about 3 miles) then turn left on Boynton Canyon Road. Proceed about 1.7 miles to a stop sign. Turn left, continuing on Boynton Pass Road. The trailhead parking is the second one on the left side, about 1.75 miles from the stop sign {1}. The trailhead is at the south side of the parking area. There are toilets at the parking area.

Description: Hike toward Doe Mountain and you'll soon intersect the Aerie Trail {2}. As you approach the rim, you'll pass through a narrow slot

28

in the rocks. Once through the slot and on the mesa, turn around and look down at the parking area. Pay attention to where you came up {3} by observing your location relative to the parking lot some 450 feet below because it can be hard to find the way back down after hiking around the top of Doe Mountain.

Although the top of Doe Mountain is crisscrossed with "social" trails, the preferred way is to proceed straight across to the southern side of Doe Mountain then proceed in a clockwise direction around then back to the trail down. Another popular way is to go to the left then skirt the outer edge of the mountain for some great views {4}{5}{6}. This way you may be bushwhacking a bit, so be sure to wear hiking boots to protect your ankles from the cactus and brush you'll be stepping over. The spectacular views are all around.

Doe Mountain Trail

Trail length (total):	2.6 miles
Trail type:	Loop
Challenge level:	Moderate
Elevation change:	525 feet

GPS Checkpoints
{1} 34°53.596'N; 111°51.945'W
{2} 34°53.545'N; 111°51.847'W
{3} 34°53.505'N; 111°51.643'W
{4} 34°53.697'N; 111°51.568'W
{5} 34°53.406'N; 111°51.572'W
{6} 34°53.288'N; 111°51.862'W

Fay Canyon Trail

Summary: A short, pleasant in-and-out stroll through a canyon with wonderful red rock formations

Challenge Level: Easy to Moderate

Hiking Distance: About 1.2 miles each way to the rock slide; 2.4 miles round trip

Trailhead Directions: From the "Y" roundabout (the intersection of State Route 89A and State Route 179), drive west toward Cottonwood on SR 89A about 3 miles. Turn right on Dry Creek Road (where speed limits are strictly enforced). Stay on Dry Creek Road (about 3 miles) to the end and a stop sign. Turn left on Boynton Canyon Road then proceed about 1.7 miles to a stop sign. Turn left, continuing on Boynton Pass Road. You park at the first parking area on the left side, about 0.8 miles from the stop sign {1}. The trailhead is across the road from the parking area.

Description: Fay Canyon is one of our favorite hikes for non-hiker guests because it is short (only about 2.4 miles round trip), relatively level, and very scenic. The trail essentially ends at a massive rock slide {4}.

There is a side trail to a natural stone arch about 0.5 mile from the main trailhead {2}. You'll have to scramble up about 225 feet on this unmarked trail if you want to see the arch, which is located up next to the cliff face {3}. This side trail is narrow with loose rock so watch your footing. There is also a narrow slot up there where the rocks have separated and you can "disappear" if you can fit into the opening. Some people suggest that the area near the arch is a powerful vortex spot.

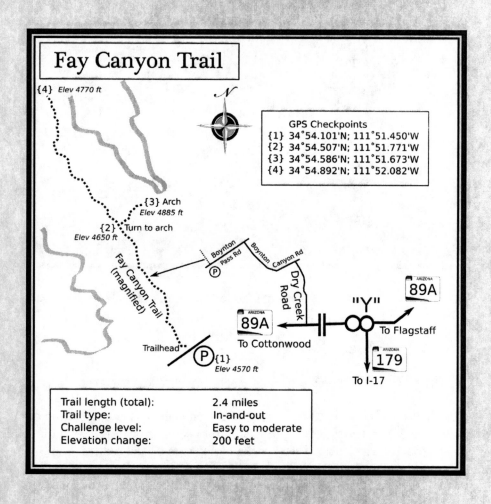

Little Horse Trail

Summary: A lovely in-and-out hike to Chicken Point, a large slickrock knoll with majestic views

Challenge Level: Moderate

Hiking Distance: About 2 miles each way; 4 miles round trip

Trailhead Directions: From the "Y" roundabout (the intersection of State Route 89A and State Route 179), drive south on SR 179 about 3.5 miles. You'll see a "Scenic View" and a hiking sign on the right side of SR 179 just past the Back 'O Beyond roundabout. Turn left here and proceed across the median to the parking area {1}. There are toilets at the parking area.

Description: You'll begin by hiking south on the Bell Rock Pathway for 0.3 mile where it intersects the beginning of the Little Horse Trail {2}. Turn left. When you come to a dry wash, turn left to cross the wash then follow the trail east then north toward the Twin Buttes, an impressive red rock formation. You will intersect the Chapel Trail at the 1.4 mile mark {3}. If you have the time, follow the Chapel Trail for 0.5 mile until it intersects Chapel Road and go up to visit the Chapel of the Holy Cross {4}. Returning to the Little Horse Trail, continue on for another 0.4 mile and you'll arrive at an expansive area of slickrock. The climb up to Chicken Point isn't hard and is well worth the effort {5}. You'll likely encounter some Pink Jeeps as the "Broken Arrow" tour brings many visitors to this beautiful area.

Little Horse Trail

To Flagstaff

ARIZONA **89A**
To Cottonwood

"Y"

ARIZONA **89A**

Elev 4480 ft {4}
Chapel

Chapel Rd

Chapel Trail

Chicken Point
{5}
Elev 4570 ft

(Back O' Beyond)

Little Horse Trail

{3}
Elev 4430 ft

ARIZONA **179**

Elev 4280 ft
Trailhead
P
P
{1}
Bell Rock Pathway

Rte 179

Turn left to
{2} Little Horse Tr
Elev 4260 ft

(Bell Rock Pathway)

To I-17

Trail length (total)	4 miles
Trail type:	In-and-out
Challenge level:	Moderate
Elevation change:	310 feet

GPS Checkpoints
{1} 34°49.433'N; 111°46.555'W
{2} 34°49.301'N; 111°46.308'W
{3} 34°49.705'N; 111°45.489'W
{4} 34°49.921'N; 111°45.938'W
{5} 34°49.794'N; 111°45.240'W

Secret Canyon Trail

Summary: An in-and-out hike up a beautiful red rock canyon

Challenge Level: Moderate

Hiking Distance: About 2.4 miles each way; 4.8 miles round trip

Trailhead Directions: From the "Y" roundabout (the intersection of State Route 89A and State Route 179), drive west toward Cottonwood on SR 89A about 3 miles. Turn right on Dry Creek Road (where speed limits are strictly enforced). Stay on Dry Creek Road for 2 miles then turn right on Forest Road (FR) 152. Proceed on FR 152 for 3.4 miles to the parking area on your left {1}. NOTE: FR 152 is an extremely rough road beyond the 0.2 mile of paved section so a high clearance vehicle is recommended.

Description: This hike goes up a very picturesque canyon. There isn't much shade until you hike about 1 mile. You'll encounter the HS Trail about 0.7 mile into the hike {2} and the David Miller Trail about 2 miles into the hike {3}. At about 2.25 miles you'll be in a pine forest. Look to your left for a deep wash and follow the wash to the right for a short

34

distance. If you are lucky, you may see a seasonal waterfall {4}. We usually stop after hiking 2.4 miles, but the trail continues on another 2 miles, becoming steeper and rockier.

Secret Canyon Trail

David Miller Trail

{3}
Elev 4940 ft

{4}
Elev 4900 ft

Secret Canyon Trail

HS Cyn

{2}
Elev 4720 ft

GPS Checklist
{1} 34°55.797'N; 111°48.391'W
{2} 34°56.299'N; 111°48.631'W
{3} 34°57.111'N; 111°49.211'W
{4} 34°56.971'N; 111°49.484'W

Trailhead
Elev 4660 ft

(magnified)

Trailhead
{1}

FR 152

Dry Creek Road

ARIZONA
89A

"Y"

ARIZONA
89A

To Flagstaff

To Cottonwood

ARIZONA
179

To I-17

Trail length (total):	4.8 miles
Trail type:	In-and-out
Challenge level:	Moderate
Elevation change:	200 feet

Soldier Pass Trail

A FAVORITE HIKE

Summary: An in-and-out hike with stops at the Devil's Kitchen and the Seven Sacred Pools with views of some impressive red rock arches

Challenge Level: Moderate

Hiking Distance: About 1.5 miles each way, 3 miles round trip; about 2.5 miles one way to the Brins Mesa Trail; 5 miles round trip

Trailhead Directions: From the "Y" roundabout (the intersection of State Route 89A and State Route 179), drive west toward Cottonwood on SR 89A for 1.25 miles then turn right on Soldier Pass Road. Proceed on Soldier Pass for 1.5 miles. Turn right on Rim Shadows. Go approximately 0.25 mile then turn left into the parking area {1}. The gate to the parking area is open from 8:00 am to 6:00 pm. If you get back to your car after 6:00 pm, you won't be able to drive out of the parking area.

Description: Shortly after beginning the Soldier Pass Trail, you'll descend into a deep wash then climb up and arrive at the Devil's Kitchen (about 0.2 mile) {2}. This is the largest sinkhole in the Sedona area. After another 0.4 mile, you'll come to the Seven Sacred Pools, which are small depressions in the red rock that hold water even in dry periods {3}. These two areas are very popular with visitors on jeep rides and hikers. You won't encounter jeeps or as many other hikers on the rest of the trail. About 1.3 miles from the trailhead, look to the right for a view of the Soldier Pass Arches {4}. As you continue, the trail becomes rockier and steeper as it climbs up to the end at Brins Mesa; about 2.5 miles from the trailhead {5}. You can return to the parking area via the jeep trail but the views aren't as nice as from the hiking trail.

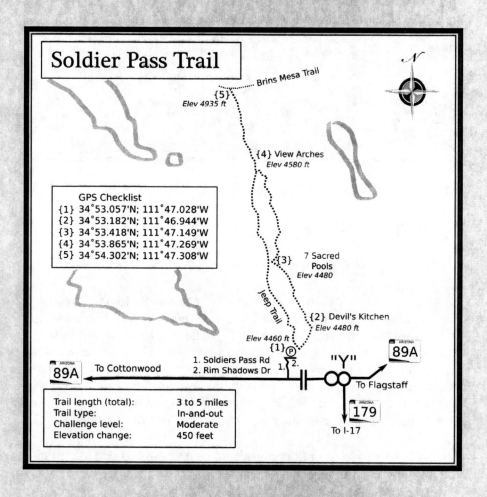

West Fork Trail

Summary: A shady in-and-out hike along a flowing creek

Challenge Level: Moderate

Hiking Distance: About 3.3 miles each way; 6.6 miles round trip

Trailhead Directions: From the "Y" roundabout (the intersection of State Route 89A and State Route 179), drive north on SR 89A about 10.5 miles. Turn left in to the parking area {1}. The trail starts on the far side of the parking area, furthest away from the entrance. There are toilets at the parking area. The gate to the parking area opens at 8:00 a.m.: use a prepay envelope if the parking attendant isn't on duty yet. The parking area fills quickly so be there early in the morning. Be sure to check on the current closing time so that your vehicle isn't trapped by the locked gates.

Description: West Fork is considered by many to be the most beautiful trail in the Sedona area. West Fork is a special fee area (see Required Parking Pass, page 14). You'll be crossing the water 13 times as you hike the trail, so bring your hiking poles. You have to step from stone to stone to cross, so the hike isn't recommended in high water times (you'll get your feet wet!!). After 0.3 mile you'll come to the remains of Mayhew's Lodge, built in the 1880s. It was remodeled in 1895 then burned down in 1980 {2}. At the 0.4 mile, mark you'll come to the first of the 13 creek crossings {3}. As you continue along, look to the sides for some amazing red rock bluffs. There is a nice spot to stop after 1 mile {4}. Just across the 10th creek crossing is a natural stone "bench" which is another nice place to stop and rest. At 2.2 miles, you'll come to a huge overhang where the water has eroded the rock {5}. Continue another 0.2 mile and watch for a short side trail to a cave on your left {6}. At 3.3 miles you'll effectively come to the end of the trail because you'll have to wade through the water to continue {7}.

West Fork has two wonderful seasons, spring and fall. The most beautiful is fall, when the deciduous trees display glorious colors. The third week in October seems to be when the colors are usually at their peak.

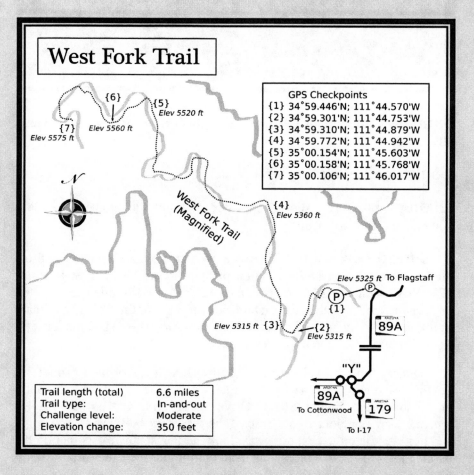

West Fork Trail

{6}
{5}
Elev 5520 ft
{7}   Elev 5560 ft
Elev 5575 ft

GPS Checkpoints
{1} 34°59.446'N; 111°44.570'W
{2} 34°59.301'N; 111°44.753'W
{3} 34°59.310'N; 111°44.879'W
{4} 34°59.772'N; 111°44.942'W
{5} 35°00.154'N; 111°45.603'W
{6} 35°00.158'N; 111°45.768'W
{7} 35°00.106'N; 111°46.017'W

West Fork Trail (Magnified)

{4}
Elev 5360 ft

Elev 5325 ft To Flagstaff
P
{1}

Elev 5315 ft {3}   {2}
Elev 5315 ft

89A

"Y"

89A
To Cottonwood   179

To I-17

Trail length (total)	6.6 miles
Trail type:	In-and-out
Challenge level:	Moderate
Elevation change:	350 feet

Best of the Rest
Airport Loop Trail

Summary: A loop hike that circles the Sedona Airport with nice views all around

Challenge Level: Easy to Moderate

Hiking Distance: About 3.25 miles total, but add another 1.0 mile if you hike the Tabletop Trail

Trailhead Directions: There are two ways to access this trail. From the "Y" roundabout (the intersection of State Route 89A and State Route 179), drive west toward Cottonwood on SR 89A for 1.0 mile then turn left on Airport Road, which is the first traffic light west of the "Y." The primary trailhead is located approximately 0.5 mile up Airport Road on the left {1}. There is parking for about a dozen vehicles here.

A secondary trailhead is located on Shelby Drive {5}, for the Bandit Trail. Shelby Drive is approximately 1.5 miles west of the "Y." Turn left (south) on Shelby Drive. Follow Shelby Drive for 0.6 mile and go past Stanley Steamer Drive on your right. Go past the two story building on your right and turn right into the next driveway. Park in the southwest corner of the parking lot {5}. Hike the Bandit Trail until it intersects the Airport Loop

Trail {4}. Continue in a clockwise direction on the Airport Loop Trail. Using the Bandit Trail to get to the Airport Loop Trail will add about 1.0 mile to your hike.

Description: As you hike around Airport Mesa below the Sedona Airport, there are good views all around. The sun on the south side of this circular hike makes photographs a challenge. On the east, there are great views of Twin Buttes and, to the south, Cathedral Rock. Be sure to hike the 0.5 mile Tabletop Trail at the southwest end of the runway {2} to the end of the mesa {3}, for a spectacular view of Sedona's pyramid. Return to the Airport Loop Trail for nice views of Chimney Rock, Capital Butte and Coffeepot Rock on the north side of the loop.

Note: The Airport Loop Trail is very rocky and there are steep drop-offs on the south side of Airport Mesa. Don't attempt this hike if a narrow trail and steep drop-offs are a concern.

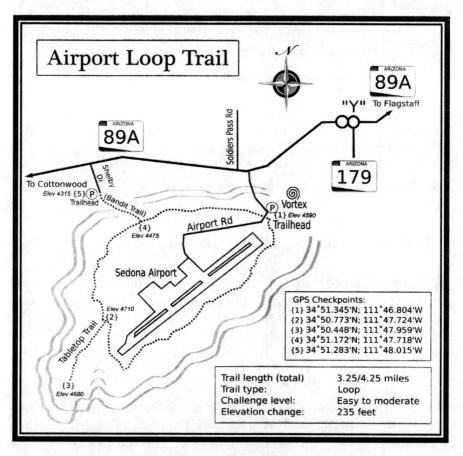

GPS Checkpoints:
{1} 34°51.345'N; 111°46.804'W
{2} 34°50.773'N; 111°47.724'W
{3} 34°50.448'N; 111°47.959'W
{4} 34°51.172'N; 111°47.718'W
{5} 34°51.283'N; 111°48.015'W

Trail length (total)	3.25/4.25 miles
Trail type:	Loop
Challenge level:	Easy to moderate
Elevation change:	235 feet

Airport Vortex Trail

Summary: Not a hike so much as it is a bit of an in-and-out scramble to the vortex located next to Airport Mesa

Challenge Level: Easy in distance, but you need to hike up a steep trail

Hiking Distance: Less than 0.25 mile round trip

Trailhead Directions: From the "Y" roundabout (the intersection of State Route 89A and State Route 179), drive west toward Cottonwood on SR 89A for 1.0 mile then turn left on Airport Road, which is the first traffic light west of the "Y." The trailhead is located approximately 0.5 mile up Airport Road on the left {1}. There is parking for about a dozen vehicles here.

Description: Your destination is "Overlook Point." From the parking area on Airport Road, you'll see a red rock formation to the left (which is your destination) and Airport Mesa to the right. Continue past the first sign and follow the main trail east until you come to a second sign in about 200 feet {2}. Turn left here and follow the trail to "Overlook Point" for a short distance and make a right turn to climb up to the overlook {3}. The top of the rock formation is "Overlook Point" and is considered to be the vortex {4}. From the overlook you have nice views of Bell Rock and Courthouse Butte to the south and Coffeepot Rock to the northwest.

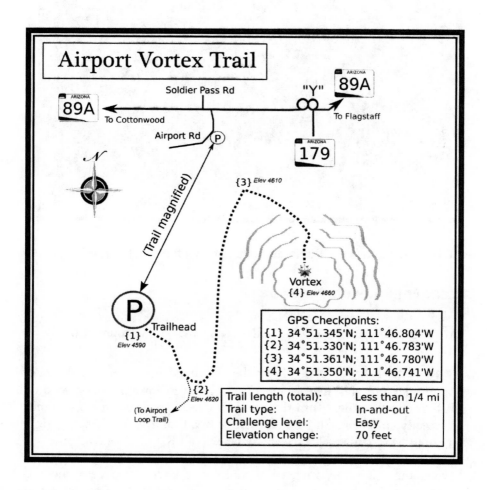

Bear Sign Trail

Summary: A beautiful, in-and-out hike in a forested red rock canyon

Challenge Level: Moderate

Hiking Distance: About 3 miles each way; 6 miles round trip

Trailhead Directions: From the "Y" roundabout (the intersection of State Route 89A and State Route 179), drive west toward Cottonwood on SR 89A about 3 miles. Turn right on Dry Creek Road (where speed limits are strictly enforced). Stay on Dry Creek Road for 2 miles then turn right on Forest Road (FR) 152. Proceed to the end of FR 152 (about 4.5 miles) to the parking area on the left {1}. NOTE: FR 152 is an extremely rough road beyond the 0.2 mile of paved section so a high clearance vehicle is recommended. The parking area is the same as used for the Dry Creek and Vultee Arch trails.

Description: After you park, proceed in a northwesterly direction on the Dry Creek Trail. You'll be hiking in the forest so there is shade. The trail is relatively flat and you'll seldom see other hikers on it. After about 0.6 mile, you'll come to a fork where the Dry Creek Trail goes to the right and the Bear Sign Trail begins to the left {2}. Grizzly bears reportedly roamed the area until the 1930s; you may actually see signs of black bear along the trail – we have! Hike some 2.8 miles to the intersection of the David Miller Trail {3}. A short, but steep hike up the David Miller Trail about 0.2 mile provides a lovely view from the saddle of the ridge between Bear Sign and Secret Canyons {4}.

Bell Rock Vortex

Summary: Explore the north side of Bell Rock on this in-and-out hike, where you may experience some vortex energy

Challenge Level: Easy to Moderate

Hiking Distance: About 0.5 mile each way; 1 mile round trip to Bell Rock: you can easily double this distance if you explore Bell Rock

Trailhead Directions: From the "Y" roundabout (the intersection of State Route 89A and State Route 179), drive south on SR 179 for about 5 miles to the parking area. After you drive about 3.2 miles, you'll come to the Back O' Beyond roundabout. SR 179 becomes a divided highway just south of the Back O' Beyond roundabout. Continue driving south. About 1.8 miles beyond the Back O' Beyond roundabout, southbound SR 179 adds a passing lane. From the passing lane, turn left at the sign for the "Court House Vista" parking area {1} (it's the second scenic view on the left side of SR 179). You'll see Bell Rock ahead of you on the left side of SR 179. There ae toilets at the parking area. If you continue driving south on SR 179, in 1 mile you'll come to the "Bell Rock Vista" parking area on your left. But if you park here, you'll need to hike north 1 mile because the south side of Bell Rock is too steep to hike or climb safely.

Description: There are many paths to explore the 600-foot-tall Bell Rock. After you park in the Court House Vista parking area, walk past the interpretive signboard and proceed straight ahead on the Bell Rock Trail. Follow it for 0.1 mile to the intersection with the Courthouse Butte Loop Trail {2}. From here you can continue straight ahead on the Bell Rock Trail to explore the northeast side of Bell Rock. Or you can turn right and follow the Courthouse Butte Loop Trail for 500 feet to a signpost on your left. Turn left here {3} and begin climbing up toward Bell Rock. Count the rock cairns along the trail and between the 10th and 11th cairn you encounter, make a sharp right turn {4}. Continue west, then south on the large flat rock shelf. Ahead you'll see where you begin climbing to the Meditation Perch {5}. You'll have to do a bit of scrambling to reach the Meditation Perch, but the climb is worth the effort. This is one of many areas on Bell Rock where people have reported feeling the earth's energy. In any case you'll enjoy a wonderful view from the Meditation Perch.

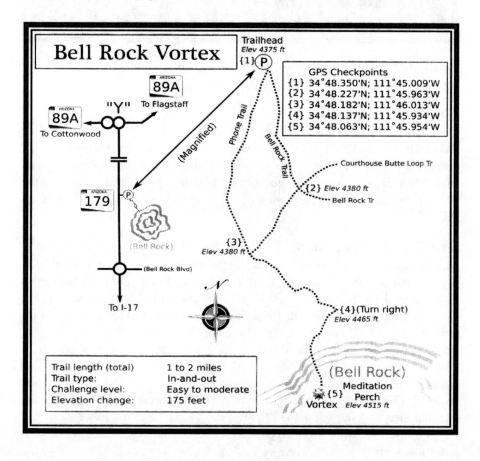

Brins Mesa Trail

Summary: An in-and-out hike to the top of a beautiful mesa with red rock views all around; or a two vehicle hike

Challenge Level: Moderate

Hiking Distance: This hike has two trailheads, one located in-town and the second off Forest Road (FR) 152. From the in-town trailhead, you'll hike 1.5 miles one way to the mesa top. If you hike west and down to the second trailhead, you'll hike another 2.4 miles for a total round trip of 7.8 miles.

Trailhead Directions: To access the in-town trailhead, from the "Y" roundabout (the intersection of State Route 89A and State Route 179), drive north on SR 89A about 0.3 mile to Jordan Road. Turn left on Jordan Road then drive to the end. Turn left on Park Ridge Drive then proceed through the paved cul-de-sac, continuing on the dirt road for 0.5 mile to the parking area {1}. There are toilets at the parking area.

To access the second trailhead off FR 152, from the "Y" roundabout, drive west on SR 89A toward Cottonwood about 3 miles. Turn right on Dry Creek Road (where speed limits are strictly enforced). Stay on Dry Creek Road for 2 miles then turn right on FR 152. Proceed for 2.5 miles to the parking area on your right {4}. NOTE: FR 152 is an extremely rough road beyond the 0.2 mile of paved section so a high clearance vehicle is recommended.

Description: The in-town trail begins on the west side of the parking area and as you begin the hike up to Brins Mesa, you are rewarded with some outstanding views. There isn't much shade on this hike so it will be hot in the summer. You'll be hiking up about 575 feet from the parking area and the trail becomes steeper as you approach the mesa. Once you reach it {2}, you'll enjoy views all around. Look to the right for the trail to the Brins Mesa Overlook (see Brins Mesa Overlook Trail on page 22). Continue straight ahead to hike to the second trailhead on FR 152, which is about another 2.4 miles away. In about 1 mile, you'll intersect the Soldier Pass Trail {3}.

Hiking from the trailhead on FR 152 is a pleasant, moderate uphill hike through trees. If possible, you may want to do this hike with two vehicles, one parked at each trailhead.

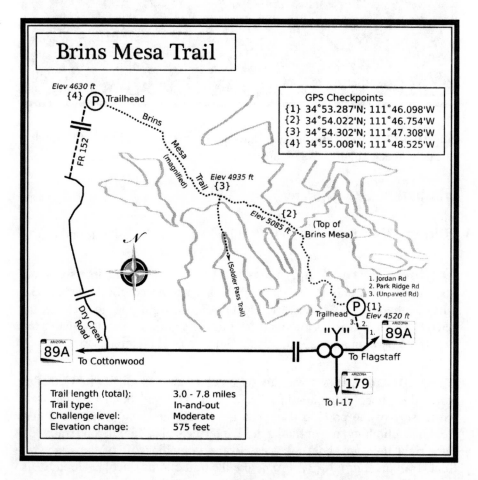

Brins Mesa Trail

Elev 4630 ft
{4} (P) Trailhead

Brins

FR 152

Mesa Trail (magnified)

Elev 4935 ft
{3}

Elev 5085 ft
{2}
(Top of Brins Mesa)

(Soldier Pass Trail)

N

GPS Checkpoints
{1} 34°53.287'N; 111°46.098'W
{2} 34°54.022'N; 111°46.754'W
{3} 34°54.302'N; 111°47.308'W
{4} 34°55.008'N; 111°48.525'W

1. Jordan Rd
2. Park Ridge Rd
3. (Unpaved Rd)

Trailhead (P) {1}
Elev 4520 ft
3. 2.
ARIZONA
"Y"
1.
ARIZONA 89A

Dry Creek Road

ARIZONA 89A

To Cottonwood

To Flagstaff

ARIZONA 179

To I-17

Trail length (total):	3.0 - 7.8 miles
Trail type:	In-and-out
Challenge level:	Moderate
Elevation change:	575 feet

Cathedral Rock Trail

Summary: A steep, sunny in-and-out hike to the "saddle" of Cathedral Rock for spectacular views all around

Challenge Level: Hard

Hiking Distance: About 0.75 miles each way; 1.5 miles round trip

Trailhead Directions: From the "Y" roundabout (the intersection of State Route 89A and State Route 179), drive south on SR 179 about 3.2 miles to the Back O' Beyond roundabout. Turn right and go west on the Back O' Beyond Road for about 0.75 mile. The parking area is on your left {1}. If the parking area is full, see the Baldwin or HT Trail description

Description: If you want to get up close and personal with Cathedral Rock, this short, strenuous hike is for you. The trail begins on the right (west) side of the parking area. You'll start out crossing a dry creek bed. Continue climbing up until the trail intersects the Templeton Trail {2}. Turn right then go about 60 paces to the branching off of the Cathedral Rock Trail on your left {3}. From here the trail climbs steeply. Good boots are recommended. Once you arrive at the saddle of Cathedral Rock {4}, you are at the location of one of four main vortex sites in Sedona. There are short trails along the south side of the east and west rock formations that lead to some good views, although the footing can be tricky. Note: If heights or tenuous footing bothers you, or the trail is wet or snowy, we do not recommend this trail.

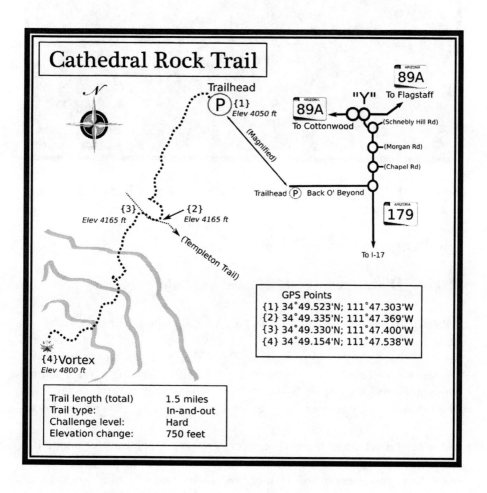

Cathedral Rock Trail

Trailhead
(P) {1}
Elev 4050 ft

89A
To Cottonwood

"Y" To Flagstaff

(Schnebly Hill Rd)

(Morgan Rd)

(Chapel Rd)

(Magnified)

Trailhead (P) Back O' Beyond

179

To I-17

{3}
Elev 4165 ft

{2}
Elev 4165 ft

(Templeton Trail)

{4} Vortex
Elev 4800 ft

GPS Points
{1} 34°49.523'N; 111°47.303'W
{2} 34°49.335'N; 111°47.369'W
{3} 34°49.330'N; 111°47.400'W
{4} 34°49.154'N; 111°47.538'W

Trail length (total)	1.5 miles
Trail type:	In-and-out
Challenge level:	Hard
Elevation change:	750 feet

Chimney Rock Loop Trail

Summary: A loop hike around the base of Chimney Rock with panoramic views

Challenge Level: Moderate

Hiking Distance: About 2.25 miles round trip

Trailhead Directions: From the "Y" roundabout (the intersection of State Route 89A and State Route 179), drive west toward Cottonwood on SR 89A about 3 miles. Turn right on Dry Creek Road (where speed limits are strictly enforced) and proceed for 0.7 mile. Turn right on Thunder Mountain Road then drive 0.6 mile. The parking area is on your left {1}. The entrance gate opens each day at 8:00 a.m.; the exit gate is never closed.

Description: From the parking area, go west on the trail for about 100 feet then turn right on the Thunder Mountain Trail. In 0.1 miles you'll come to the intersection of Thunder Mountain and Chimney Rock Trails {2}. Turn right here. We prefer to hike around the base of Chimney Rock in the counterclockwise direction because the steep trail on the northeast side is easier (and safer) to hike uphill versus going downhill. As you circle Chimney Rock, you'll have panoramic views of the mountains around

Sedona and you'll intersect the Andante {3}, Lizard Head {8}, and Lower Chimney Trails {10}. After 0.6 mile, the Thunder Mountain Trail goes off to the right {4}. At the 0.8 mile mark, you'll see a fencepost on your right {5}. About 50 feet past the fencepost, the more adventurous can turn right to take a short, steep side trail up to an overlook {6}; it's a scramble but worth it for the view. About 180 feet past the fencepost is another unmarked trail {7} to the left, another scramble, which leads to the "chimney" of Chimney Rock. Continuing on, at 1.4 miles you'll intersect a steep trail, which leads to the summit on Little Sugarloaf {10}; stay left to complete the Chimney Rock Loop.

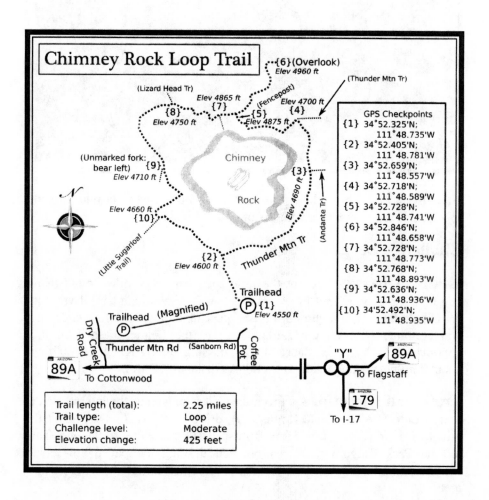

Chimney Rock Loop Trail

{6} (Overlook)
Elev 4960 ft

(Thunder Mtn Tr)

(Lizard Head Tr)
Elev 4865 ft
{7}
{8}
Elev 4750 ft

(Fencepost)
Elev 4700 ft
{5}
Elev 4875 ft
{4}

Chimney

Rock

(Unmarked fork: bear left) {9}
Elev 4710 ft

Elev 4660 ft
{10}

(Andante Tr)
Elev 4690 ft

(Little Sugarloaf Trail)

{3}

Thunder Mtn Tr

{2}
Elev 4600 ft

Trailhead

Trailhead (Magnified)
(P) {1}
Elev 4550 ft

(P)
Dry Creek Road
Thunder Mtn Rd (Sanborn Rd)
Coffee Pot

"Y"
ARIZONA
89A
To Flagstaff

ARIZONA
89A
To Cottonwood

ARIZONA
179
To I-17

GPS Checkpoints
{1} 34°52.325'N;
     111°48.735'W
{2} 34°52.405'N;
     111°48.781'W
{3} 34°52.659'N;
     111°48.557'W
{4} 34°52.718'N;
     111°48.589'W
{5} 34°52.728'N;
     111°48.741'W
{6} 34°52.846'N;
     111°48.658'W
{7} 34°52.728'N;
     111°48.773'W
{8} 34°52.768'N;
     111°48.893'W
{9} 34°52.636'N;
     111°48.936'W
{10} 34°52.492'N;
     111°48.935'W

Trail length (total):	2.25 miles
Trail type:	Loop
Challenge level:	Moderate
Elevation change:	425 feet

Cibola Pass Trail

Summary: This close-to-town, in-and-out hike provides some spectacular red rock views with the option to hike a loop

Challenge Level: Moderate

Hiking Distance: About 0.8 mile each way; 1.6 miles round trip if you hike the Cibola Trail in-and-out. About 2 miles round trip, if you hike the Cibola Pass Trail then return to the parking area via the Jordan Trail. If you continue west on the Jordan Trail to the Soldier Pass Trail then continue on to the Seven Sacred Pools, passing Devil's Kitchen, you'll add about 2 miles, making the total round trip distance 4 miles.

Trailhead Directions: From the "Y" roundabout (the intersection of State Route 89A and State Route 179), drive north on SR 89A about 0.3 mile to Jordan Road. Turn left on Jordan Road then drive to the end. Turn left on Park Ridge Drive then proceed through the paved cul-de-sac, continuing on the dirt road for 0.5 mile {1}. There are toilets at the parking area.

Description: Begin hiking the trail on the west side of the parking area near the toilets. The Cibola Pass trail branches left from the Brins Mesa trail after about 400 feet {2}. The trail is quite steep in places. As you proceed, you'll have some very nice red rock views. At about 0.6 mile, you'll approach two fence posts on the left side {3}. If you go straight for a short distance, you'll have some great views. Return to the fence posts then continue on the trail. You'll meet the Jordan Trail after hiking 0.8 mile {4}. Turn around here to return to the parking area via the Cibola Trail, or turn south and follow the Jordan Trail back to the parking area for a 2 mile loop.

Or proceed west on the Jordan Trail to the Soldier Pass Trail. Turn right on the Soldier Pass Trail, which leads to Devil's Kitchen (a very large sink hole) {5} then on to the Seven Sacred Pools {6}. You'll have hiked about 4 miles for the entire hike from the Seven Sacred Pools when you return to the parking area via the Jordan Trail.

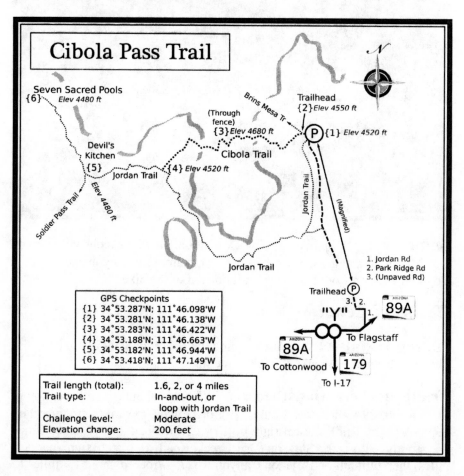

Cockscomb to Aerie Loop Trail

Summary: A loop hike circling Doe Mountain with excellent views of Doe Mountain and great views of Bear Mountain, Fay Canyon and Boynton Canyon from the Aerie Trail portion of the hike

Challenge Level: Moderate

Hiking Distance: 5.4 miles around the entire loop but if you have two vehicles you can make it a 3.75 mile hike

Trailhead Directions: From the "Y" roundabout (the intersection of State Route 89A and State Route 179), drive west toward Cottonwood on SR 89A about 3 miles. Turn right on Dry Creek Road (where speed limits are strictly enforced). Stay on Dry Creek Road to a stop sign (about 3 miles) then turn left on Boynton Canyon Road. Proceed about 1.7 miles to a stop sign. Turn left and continue on Boynton Pass Road. Drive about 2.5 miles and turn left on Aerie Road, which is about 0.5 mile past the Doe Mountain/Bear Mountain parking area on the left side of Boynton Pass Road. Follow Aerie Road and take the right fork to the parking area {1}.

Description: About 100 feet from the parking area is a trail sign. Go straight to follow the Cockscomb Trail and hike around Doe Mountain in a counter clockwise direction (which is how we hike it). You'll intersect the Rupp Trail after 1.5 miles {2}. There is a nice spot to stop for a snack after about 2 miles {3}. You'll intersect the Dawa Trail after 2.4 miles {4}. Continue on and you'll intersect the Aerie Trail after another 0.8 mile {5}. If you continue straight on the Cockscomb Trail you'll come to the Fay Canyon parking area for a 3.75 mile hike. Turn left to follow the Aerie Trail across the north side of Doe Mountain. You'll cross the trail leading up to Doe Mountain about 4.6 miles into the hike {6}. The views are much better after you hike around to the east side of Doe Mountain and begin your way back on the Aerie Trail.

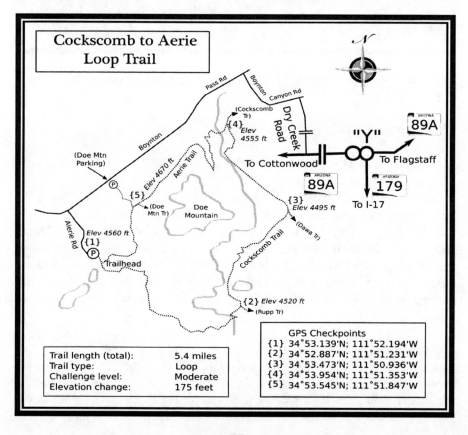

Coffeepot Trail

Summary: An in-town, in-and-out trail that takes you to the base of Coffeepot Rock

Challenge Level: Easy

Hiking Distance: About 1.2 miles each way; 2.4 miles round trip

Trailhead Directions: From the "Y" roundabout (the intersection of State Route 89A and State Route 179), drive west toward Cottonwood on SR 89A for just under 2 miles and turn right on Coffeepot Drive. Drive about 0.5 miles then turn left on Sanborn. Continue to the second street then turn right on Little Elf. Little Elf ends at Buena Vista so make a short right on Buena Vista then a quick left into the parking area {1}. This parking area also serves the Teacup, Thunder Mountain and Sugarloaf trails.

Description: About 50 feet past the interpretive signboard near the parking area, look for a sign on the right {2}. Follow the Teacup/Sugarloaf Summit Trail for 0.3 mile. Turn right at the next sign {3} and continue on the Teacup Trail. You'll soon come to a sign for the Sugarloaf Summit Loop Trail {4}. Continue on the Teacup Trail for another 0.15 mile and turn left

{5} on to an unmarked trail, that we call the Coffeepot Trail, which will lead you to the base of Coffeepot Rock. There are many "social trails" in this area so be sure to follow the cairns until you turn off on to the Coffeepot Trail. There aren't any cairns along this trail, but it is easy to follow. You'll hike on rock ledges under Coffeepot and come to Shark Rock {6}, which looks like the open mouth of a giant shark. Continue on until the ledges eventually become too narrow and steep to go any farther {7}. Return the way you came for a 2.4 mile hike.

There is little shade on this trail making this a hot summer hike.

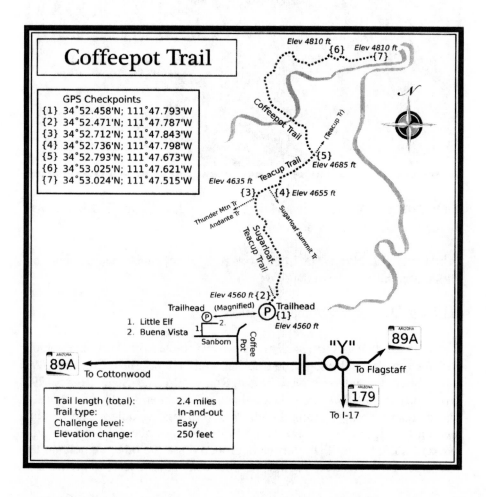

Cookstove to Harding Springs Trails

Summary: A two-vehicle hike up the side of Oak Creek Canyon, through a pine forest and down again

Challenge Level: Hard (and we strongly recommend using a portable GPS unit to hike between the two trails)

Hiking Distance: About 3.2 miles

Trailhead Directions: This is a two-vehicle hike. Park one vehicle at Cave Springs and one at the artesian well at Pine Flats. From the "Y" roundabout (the intersection of State Route 89A and State Route 179), drive north on SR 89A about 11.7 miles (mile marker 385.6) then turn left into the Cave Springs campground. Park your first vehicle in the parking area on the right {13}. Continue north on SR 89A about 1.2 miles (mile marker 386.9) to the Pine Flats campground. Park the other vehicle on the west side of SR 89A near the well {1}, but don't block access to the well.

Description: Once you park the second vehicle, cross SR 89A to the sign for the Cookstove Trail and hike up the east side of Oak Creek

Canyon. The trail is very steep with many switchbacks and climbs about 750 feet to a flat mesa. You'll find a trail marker cut into a large pine tree at the top of the trail {2}. Hike south following the edge of Oak Creek Canyon. You'll turn away from Oak Creek Canyon to skirt a side canyon, then make a series of turns {3}{4}{5}. You'll cross several washes and hike along an old road, then rejoin the trail and intersect the Harding Springs Trail {6}{7}{8}{9}{10}. Before starting down the steep Harding Springs Trail (to your other vehicle), continue about 450 feet south along the canyon rim to a nice overlook area {11}. The unmarked, unmaintained trail is difficult to follow at times, and is not a straight line between the top of the Cookstove Trail and the Harding Springs Trail. Also, you'll be climbing over many fallen trees. We strongly recommend using a portable GPS unit to hike between the trails across the mesa (see page 7). This is a shady hike in the summer, with good foliage colors in the fall. Do not attempt if there is snow on the trail.

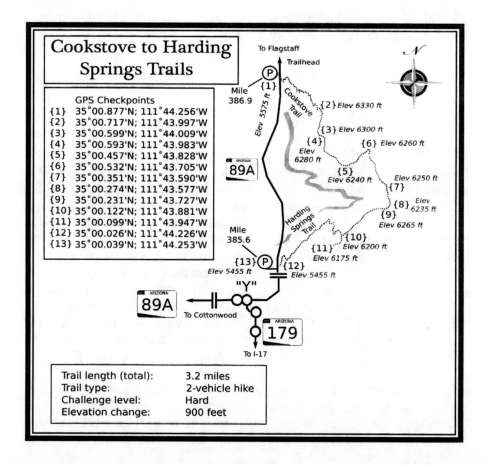

Cookstove to Harding Springs Trails

GPS Checkpoints
{1}	35°00.877'N; 111°44.256'W
{2}	35°00.717'N; 111°43.997'W
{3}	35°00.599'N; 111°44.009'W
{4}	35°00.593'N; 111°43.983'W
{5}	35°00.457'N; 111°43.828'W
{6}	35°00.532'N; 111°43.705'W
{7}	35°00.351'N; 111°43.590'W
{8}	35°00.274'N; 111°43.577'W
{9}	35°00.231'N; 111°43.727'W
{10}	35°00.122'N; 111°43.881'W
{11}	35°00.099'N; 111°43.947'W
{12}	35°00.026'N; 111°44.226'W
{13}	35°00.039'N; 111°44.253'W

Trail length (total): 3.2 miles
Trail type: 2-vehicle hike
Challenge level: Hard
Elevation change: 900 feet

Courthouse Butte Loop Trail

Summary: A pleasant loop hike circling Bell Rock and Courthouse Butte near the Village of Oak Creek

Challenge Level: Moderate

Hiking Distance: About 4.3 miles round trip

Trailhead Directions: There are two trailhead parking areas for this hike, both along State Route 179. From the "Y" roundabout (the intersection of State Route 89A and State Route 179), drive south on SR 179 for about 5 miles to the parking area. After you drive about 3.2 miles, you'll come to the Back O' Beyond roundabout. SR 179 becomes a divided highway just south of the Back O' Beyond roundabout. Continue driving south. About 1.8 miles beyond the Back O' Beyond roundabout, southbound SR 179 adds a passing lane. From the passing lane, turn left at the sign for the "Court House Vista" parking area {1} (it's the second scenic view on the left side of SR 179). You'll see Bell Rock ahead of you on the left side of SR 179. After you park, walk past the interpretive signboard and proceed straight ahead on the Bell Rock Trail. Follow it for 0.1 mile to the intersection with the Courthouse Butte Loop Trail {2}.

If you continue driving south on SR 179, in 1 mile you'll come to the "Bell Rock Vista" parking area on your left. Turn left into the parking area {8}. There are toilets at both the parking areas. Follow the Bell Rock Pathway Trail north for about 0.5 mile until you intersect the Courthouse Butte Loop Trail {7}.

Description: This trail circling Courthouse Butte and Bell Rock combines panoramic and close-up views of these two famous rock formations as well as distant views of Rabbit Ears, the Chapel of the Holy Cross and Cathedral Rock. The trail is open, providing little shade so it will be a hot summer hike. We like to hike this loop in the clockwise direction, although either direction provides great views. You'll intersect several trails as you hike including the Llama Trail {3} and Big Park Loop Trail {5}. From the Bell Rock Vista parking area, the trail starts out wide and defined by fences on both sides. A good stopping point for a snack break is near "Muffin Rock," which some call "UFO Rock" {4}.

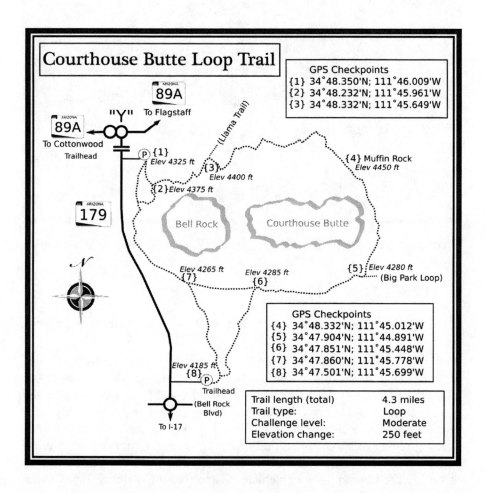

Courthouse Butte Loop Trail

GPS Checkpoints
{1} 34°48.350'N; 111°46.009'W
{2} 34°48.232'N; 111°45.961'W
{3} 34°48.332'N; 111°45.649'W

ARIZONA **89A**
"Y" To Flagstaff
(Llama Trail)

ARIZONA **89A**
To Cottonwood
Trailhead

℗ {1}
Elev 4325 ft
{3}
Elev 4400 ft
{2} Elev 4375 ft

{4} Muffin Rock
Elev 4450 ft

ARIZONA **179**

Bell Rock

Courthouse Butte

Elev 4265 ft
{7}
Elev 4285 ft
{6}
{5} Elev 4280 ft
(Big Park Loop)

Elev 4185 ft
{8}
℗
Trailhead
(Bell Rock Blvd)
To I-17

GPS Checkpoints
{4} 34°48.332'N; 111°45.012'W
{5} 34°47.904'N; 111°44.891'W
{6} 34°47.851'N; 111°45.448'W
{7} 34°47.860'N; 111°45.778'W
{8} 34°47.501'N; 111°45.699'W

Trail length (total)	4.3 miles
Trail type:	Loop
Challenge level:	Moderate
Elevation change:	250 feet

Cow Pies Trail

Summary: An in-and-out stroll over slickrock with nice views all around

Challenge Level: Easy

Hiking Distance: About 1.25 miles each way; 2.5 miles round trip

Trailhead Directions: From the "Y" roundabout (the intersection of State Route 89A and State Route 179), drive south on SR 179 about 0.3 mile to the Schnebly Hill Roundabout then drive 270 degrees (3/4 of the way) around to Schnebly Hill Road. Proceed 3.7 miles on Schnebly Hill. The trailhead parking is on your right {1}. Either park along the road (leaving plenty of room for vehicles to pass) or use the far entrance to the parking area as the near entrance is very steep and you have a good chance of hitting the bottom of your vehicle. Schnebly Hill is paved for the first mile but the last 2.7 miles can be a very rough unpaved road; a high clearance vehicle is recommended.

Description: The Cow Pies area is likely named because the four huge semi-circular sandstone mounds resemble very large cow droppings. The trailhead is across the road from the parking area. Soon you'll pass by an area dotted with small black rocks, which are pieces of lava. Some believe this to be another powerful vortex area {2}. Continue along the trail for 0.3 mile, then make a left turn {3} to go to the "cow pies." If you go straight, you'll be hiking the Mitten Ridge Trail. As you continue to the left, you'll hike up on the "cow pies," which border Bear Wallow. You'll have to do a bit of scrambling in some areas to ascend the "cow pies." There isn't a defined trail so you'll be free to explore the "cow pies." There are a number of areas that provide good views {4}{5}.

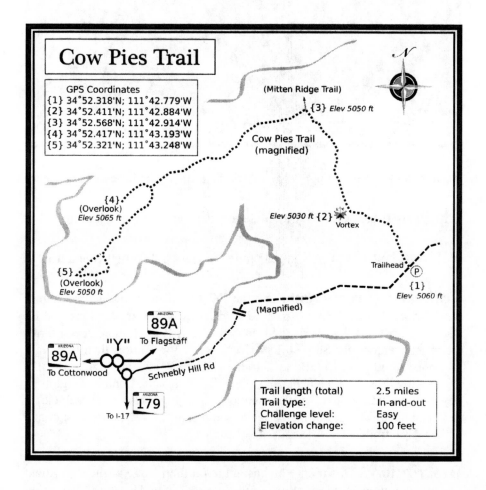

65

Dry Creek Trail

Summary: An in-and-out hike through a forest that follows Dry Creek

Challenge Level: Easy to moderate, depending on length of hike

Hiking Distance: About 2.25 miles each way, 4.5 miles round trip

Trailhead Directions: From the "Y" roundabout (the intersection of State Route 89A and State Route 179), drive west toward Cottonwood on SR 89A about 3 miles. Turn right on Dry Creek Road (where speed limits are strictly enforced). Stay on Dry Creek Road for 2 miles then turn right on Forest Road (FR) 152. Proceed to the end of FR 152 (about 4.5 miles) to the parking area on the left {1}. NOTE: FR 152 is an extremely rough road beyond the 0.2 mile of paved section so a high clearance vehicle is recommended. The parking area is the same as used for the Bear Sign and Vultee Arch trails.

Description: This trail, which is at the northern edge of the Red Rock-Secret Mountain Wilderness, follows the path cut by Dry Creek, crossing

66

the dry creek bed about a dozen times. You'll be hiking in a northerly direction and intersect the Bear Sign Trail about 0.8 mile in {2}. As you continue, the canyon cut by Dry Creek gets narrower and you are treated to nice views of towering red rock formations, although some of the views are blocked by the vegetation {3}. You can hike another 0.75 mile further up the creek bed if you like.

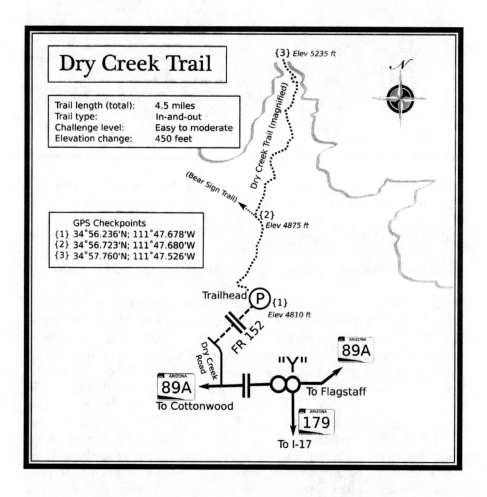

Honanki Heritage Site

Summary: A loop hike to Sinagua pueblo ruins and rock art tucked under a shallow red rock overhang

Challenge Level: Easy

Hiking Distance: About 0.25 mile each way; 0.5 mile round trip

Trailhead Directions: From the "Y" roundabout (the intersection of State Route 89A and State Route 179), drive west toward Cottonwood on SR 89A about 3 miles. Turn right on Dry Creek Road (where speed limits are strictly enforced) {1}. Stay on Dry Creek Road to a stop sign (about 3 miles) then turn left on Boynton Canyon Road {2}. Proceed about 1.7 miles to a stop sign. Turn left, continuing on Boynton Pass Road {3}. The first 2 miles is paved, then becomes a gravel road. Drive 4 miles to a stop sign then turn right on Forest Road (FR) 525 {4}. After about 0.1 mile take the left fork of FR 525 {5} then continue for another 4.5 miles to the parking area {7}. On the way you'll see a faint road off to the left {6} which leads to the Bradshaw Overlook – an area with good panoramic views. Note: this unpaved road can be very rough so a high clearance vehicle is recommended.

Description: The Sinagua, ancestors of the Hopi, lived at Honanki from about AD 1100 to 1300. Here they prepared meals, raised their families, and made tools from stone, leather, and wood. They hunted for deer and rabbit, tended various crops, and gathered edible wild plants nearby.

The Pink Jeep Company manages the Honanki (meaning Bear House) site so there are no volunteers or rangers stationed at this site (like at Palatki). You are on your own to wander through the site. There is a metal rail fence to keep unauthorized folks out but you are very close to the structures. You likely will encounter people touring the site who are on jeep tours at the time you are there. The Pink Jeep Company asks that you not interfere with the tours.

The only facilities at Honanki are toilets. Pets are not allowed on the site.

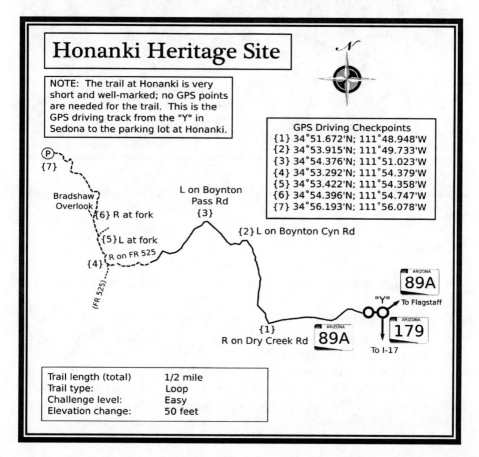

Honanki Heritage Site

NOTE: The trail at Honanki is very short and well-marked; no GPS points are needed for the trail. This is the GPS driving track from the "Y" in Sedona to the parking lot at Honanki.

GPS Driving Checkpoints
{1} 34°51.672'N; 111°48.948'W
{2} 34°53.915'N; 111°49.733'W
{3} 34°54.376'N; 111°51.023'W
{4} 34°53.292'N; 111°54.379'W
{5} 34°53.422'N; 111°54.358'W
{6} 34°54.396'N; 111°54.747'W
{7} 34°56.193'N; 111°56.078'W

P
{7}

Bradshaw
Overlook
{6} R at fork

L on Boynton
Pass Rd
{3}

{5} L at fork

{2} L on Boynton Cyn Rd

R on FR 525
{4}

(FR 525)

ARIZONA
89A

"Y" To Flagstaff

{1}
R on Dry Creek Rd

ARIZONA
89A

ARIZONA
179

To I-17

Trail length (total)	1/2 mile
Trail type:	Loop
Challenge level:	Easy
Elevation change:	50 feet

HS Canyon Trail

Summary: A pleasant in-and-out hike through a narrow, forested canyon

Challenge Level: Moderate

Hiking Distance: About 2 miles each way; 4 miles round trip

Trailhead Directions: From the "Y" roundabout (the intersection of State Route 89A and State Route 179), drive west toward Cottonwood on SR 89A about 3 miles. Turn right on Dry Creek Road (where speed limits are strictly enforced). Stay on Dry Creek Road for 2 miles then turn right on Forest Road (FR) 152. Proceed on FR 152 for 3.4 miles to the parking area on your left {1}. NOTE: FR 152 is an extremely rough road beyond the 0.2 mile of paved section so a high clearance vehicle is recommended.

Description: To reach the HS Trail, you begin hiking the Secret Canyon Trail. After about 0.7 mile, you'll see the HS Canyon Trail #50 sign on your left {2}. The trail gently rises about 600 feet providing good red rock views, although the forest of alligator junipers and oak obscures some of the views. The name originally comes from the early riders finding lots of horse s**t on this trail. When the Forest Service officially named the trail, they kept the initials (HS) but named it after Henry Schuerman, an early Sedona resident. A good hike for the hot summer as there is plenty of shade. The trail ends next to Maroon Mountain {3}.

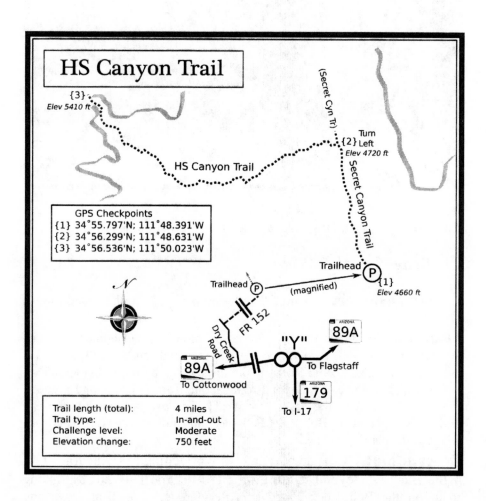

HT Trail

Summary: A partially shaded hike to the base of Cathedral Rock

Challenge Level: Moderate

Hiking Distance: About 2.75 miles each way; 5.5 miles round trip

Trailhead Directions: From the "Y" roundabout (the intersection of State Route 89A and State Route 179), drive south on SR 179 about 3.5 miles. You'll see a "Scenic View" and a hiking sign on the right side of SR 179 just past the Back O' Beyond roundabout. Turn left here and proceed across the median to the parking area {1}. The parking area for the HT Trail is the same as for Bell Rock Pathway and Little Horse Trail. There are toilets at the parking area.

Description: This is an alternate way of getting to Cathedral Rock if the Back O' Beyond parking area is full. You'll begin by hiking south on the Bell Rock Pathway. After 0.3 mile you'll intersect the beginning of the Little Horse Trail {2}. Continue south for another 0.2 mile, cross the footbridge and the HT Trail begins on your right {3}. As you hike along the HT Trail, you'll pass under both the northbound and southbound lanes of SR 179. There are Pinyon pines in this area so you are partially shaded. You follow along the wash you crossed just before turning to the HT Trail. After 1.4 miles, you'll intersect the Templeton Trail {4}. Turn right and proceed toward Cathedral Rock.

As you approach Cathedral Rock, the landscape changes to a desert environment and you'll see Ocotillo plants, which likely will have their red blooms displayed in mid to late April. Continue west along the Templeton Trail and you'll intersect the Cathedral Rock Trail coming up from the parking area on the Back O' Beyond Road {5}. From here you can scramble up to the "saddle" of Cathedral Rock (see Cathedral Rock Trail).

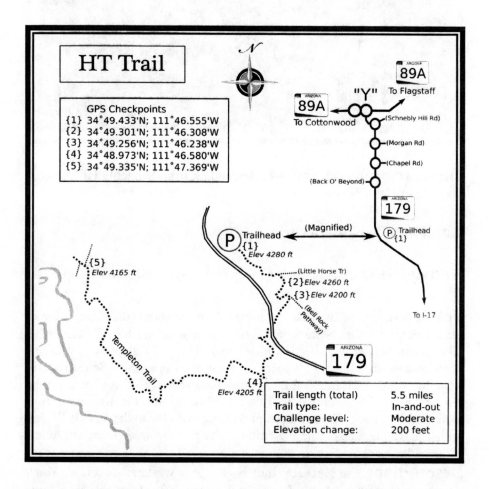

Huckaby Trail

Summary: An in-and-out hike descending from Schnebly Hill Road to the bank of Oak Creek

Challenge Level: Moderate

Hiking Distance: About 2.5 miles each way; 5 miles round trip

Trailhead Directions: From the "Y" roundabout (the intersection of State Route 89A and State Route 179), drive south on SR 179 about 0.3 mile to the Schnebly Hill roundabout then drive 270 degrees (3/4 of the way) around to Schnebly Hill Road. Proceed on the paved Schnebly Hill Road for 1 mile then turn left into the parking area {1}. If you start driving on the unpaved Schnebly Hill Road, you've missed the trailhead. Turn around and go back. The trailhead parking is shared with the Munds Wagon trail. The trail begins on the west side of the parking area. There are toilets at the parking area.

Description: The Huckaby trail begins in a westerly direction. You'll shortly intersect the Marg's Draw Trail to the left. Huckaby then turns north and crosses Bear Wallow Wash. The trail rises and falls as you

74

approach Oak Creek Canyon. After 1 mile, as you begin to descend to the eastern bank of Oak Creek, there is shade provided by the riparian trees {2}. You have views of "Lucy," "Snoopy," Cathedral Rock and Uptown Sedona. Soon you have a good view of Midgley Bridge {3}. Watch for poison ivy along the trail. Unless the water is low and you want to cross to the other side of Oak Creek by doing some rock-hopping {4}, end the hike where you have an awesome view of Midgley Bridge, just north of Uptown Sedona {3}.

If you continue across Oak Creek, you'll hike up about 150 feet and turn west toward Midgley Bridge. You can make this hike a two vehicle hike – one vehicle parked at the Schnebly Hill Road parking area {1} and the other parked at Midgley Bridge {5}. Just make sure you can cross Oak Creek.

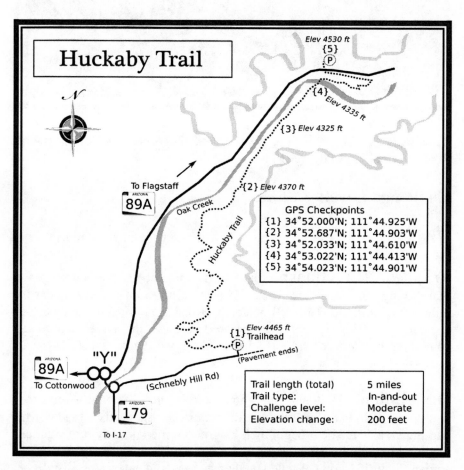

Huckaby Trail

Elev 4530 ft
{5}
{4} Elev 4335 ft
{3} Elev 4325 ft
To Flagstaff
{2} Elev 4370 ft
89A
ARIZONA
Oak Creek
Huckaby Trail

GPS Checkpoints
{1} 34°52.000'N; 111°44.925'W
{2} 34°52.687'N; 111°44.903'W
{3} 34°52.033'N; 111°44.610'W
{4} 34°53.022'N; 111°44.413'W
{5} 34°54.023'N; 111°44.901'W

Elev 4465 ft
{1} Trailhead
(Pavement ends)

"Y"
89A
ARIZONA
To Cottonwood
(Schnebly Hill Rd)
179
ARIZONA
To I-17

Trail length (total)	5 miles
Trail type:	In-and-out
Challenge level:	Moderate
Elevation change:	200 feet

Jim Thompson Trail

Summary: An in-and-out hike around the south edge of Steamboat Rock overlooking Midgley Bridge

Challenge Level: Moderate

Hiking Distance: About 2.5 miles each way; 5 miles round trip

Trailhead Directions: From the "Y" roundabout (the intersection of State Route 89A and State Route 179), drive north on SR 89A about 0.3 mile to Jordan Road. Turn left on Jordan Road then drive to the end. Turn left on Park Ridge Drive then proceed through the paved cul-de-sac, continuing on the dirt road for 0.5 mile to the parking area {1}. There are toilets at the parking area.

Description: Built by Jim Thompson in the 1880s as a road to a homestead at Indian Gardens, the trail begins on the northeast side of the parking area {2}. You'll begin by hiking north, then quickly turn right and begin hiking south. After hiking 0.4 mile, you'll intersect the end of the Jordan Trail {3}. In 0.3 mile you'll come to an old gate frame. You'll be hiking in an easterly direction along Jim Thompson's old wagon road toward the base of Steamboat Rock. There isn't much shade on this hike so it will be hot in the summer. We usually stop after about 2.5 miles where you can see the Midgley Bridge and look across Oak Creek Canyon {4}. If you continue on for about 0.25 mile, you'll intersect the Wilson Canyon Trail {5}.

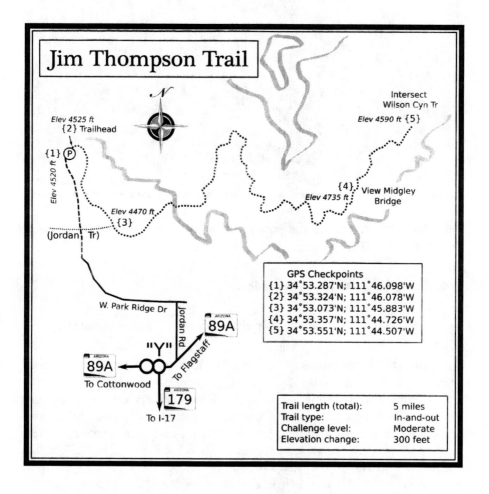

Jim Thompson Trail

N

Intersect
Wilson Cyn Tr

Elev 4590 ft {5}

Elev 4525 ft
{2} Trailhead

{1} Ⓟ
Elev 4520 ft

{4}
Elev 4735 ft View Midgley
Bridge

Elev 4470 ft
{3}

(Jordan Tr)

GPS Checkpoints		
{1} 34°53.287'N; 111°46.098'W		
{2} 34°53.324'N; 111°46.078'W		
{3} 34°53.073'N; 111°45.883'W		
{4} 34°53.357'N; 111°44.726'W		
{5} 34°53.551'N; 111°44.507'W		

W. Park Ridge Dr

Jordan Rd

ARIZONA
89A

"Y"

ARIZONA
89A ←

To Flagstaff

To Cottonwood

ARIZONA
179

To I-17

Trail length (total):	5 miles
Trail type:	In-and-out
Challenge level:	Moderate
Elevation change:	300 feet

Jordan Trail

Summary: An in-and-out partially shaded hike near town that ends at the Soldier Pass Trail

Challenge Level: Easy to moderate

Hiking Distance: About 1.4 miles each way; 2.8 miles round trip

Trailhead Directions: From the "Y" roundabout (the intersection of State Route 89A and State Route 179), drive north on SR 89A about 0.3 mile to Jordan Road. Turn left on Jordan Road then drive to the end. Turn left on Park Ridge Drive then proceed through the paved cul-de-sac, continuing on the dirt road for 0.5 mile to the parking area. There are toilets at the parking area. There are two trailheads for this trail. The trailhead at the parking area is on the west side, to the right of the toilets. If you walk back down the road 0.4 mile there is another Jordan Trail signpost {2}.

Description: If you begin the hike from the parking area, you'll hike a short distance to the west, then turn south. After 0.4 mile, you'll intersect the second Jordan Trail {3}. If you turn left (east), you'll cross the road then intersect the Jim Thompson Trail after 0.2 mile. Instead, turn right (west) then begin hiking the main trail somewhat uphill as you hike along an old road. The views gradually improve as you continue the hike. You'll intersect the Cibola Trail at the 1.1 mile mark {4}. Continue on the Jordan Trail until you intersect the Soldier Pass Trail at Devil's Kitchen, which is the largest sinkhole in the Sedona area {5}. If you want to continue a little further, hike north on the Soldier Pass Trail for 0.4 mile to the Seven Sacred Pools {6}. You can retrace your route or hike back on the Cibola Trail to the parking area. The Jordan Trail is popular with mountain bicyclists so you may encounter them on the trail.

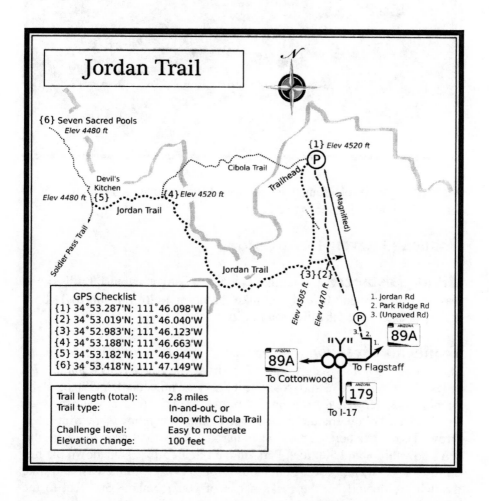

Kelly Canyon Trail

Summary: A pleasant, shaded in-and-out hike in a Ponderosa Pine forest with interesting rocks and cliffs

Challenge Level: Easy to Moderate

Hiking Distance: If you hike east Kelly Canyon about 1.3 miles each way; 2.6 miles round trip. If you hike the north Kelly Canyon trail about 2.7 miles each way; 5.5 miles round trip

Trailhead Directions: From the "Y" roundabout (the intersection of State Route 89A and State Route 179), drive north on SR 89A about 17.5 miles. Turn right on a dirt road, (FR 237) at mile marker 390.6, at an opening in a long guard rail on the right, {1} 1.5 miles beyond the Oak Creek Vista. Follow the dirt road about 1 mile to a yellow sign with a left arrow. Turn right here {2} on an unmarked faint road near the sign and drive downhill about 500 feet. Park on the flat area {3}. Hike down the hill on the left (east) and enter Pumphouse Wash {4}. Continue east and hike through the opening in the rocks ahead of you for about 500 feet to the beginning of the trail {5}. Note: the drive downhill to the parking area is extremely rough: a high clearance vehicle is required.

Description: This hike takes you across Pumphouse Wash and up Kelly Canyon which is thickly forested and shady. It is a very peaceful and beautiful hike, although you won't find red rock views here. There are interesting rock formations as you travel along. At 0.6 mile you'll make a left turn and climb down into the wash {6} to follow the trail. After 1 mile, you'll intersect a faint trail on the right that follows what we call East Kelly Canyon {7}. You'll need to do a bit of bushwhacking if you hike this trail {8}. If you continue straight you'll follow a well-marked trail along a wash we call North Kelly Canyon. You'll come to a ramp over a downed tree after another 0.3 mile {9}. You'll intersect several social trails along the way {10} {11}. After hiking a total of 2.7 miles, you'll intersect FR 237 {12}.

The ambient temperature you encounter on this hike will be cooler than in Sedona because of the elevation (about 6400 feet) and the shade provided by the trees. It is a pleasant summer hike, but watch for poison ivy.

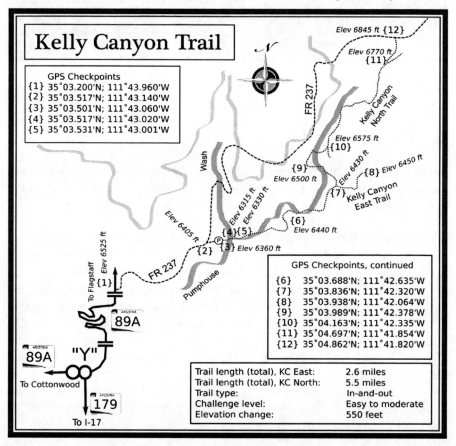

Kelly Canyon Trail

GPS Checkpoints
{1} 35°03.200'N; 111°43.960'W
{2} 35°03.517'N; 111°43.140'W
{3} 35°03.501'N; 111°43.060'W
{4} 35°03.517'N; 111°43.020'W
{5} 35°03.531'N; 111°43.001'W

Elev 6845 ft {12}
Elev 6770 ft {11}
FR 237
Kelly Canyon North Trail
Elev 6575 ft {10}
Wash
Elev 6630 ft
{9} Elev 6500 ft
Elev 6315 ft
Elev 6330 ft
{8} Elev 6450 ft
{7} Kelly Canyon East Trail
Elev 6405 ft
{4}{5}
{2} {3} Elev 6360 ft
{6} Elev 6440 ft
Pumphouse
To Flagstaff Elev 6525 ft
{1}
FR 237
89A
89A "Y"
To Cottonwood
179
To I-17

GPS Checkpoints, continued
{6}   35°03.688'N; 111°42.635'W
{7}   35°03.836'N; 111°42.320'W
{8}   35°03.938'N; 111°42.064'W
{9}   35°03.989'N; 111°42.378'W
{10} 35°04.163'N; 111°42.335'W
{11} 35°04.697'N; 111°41.854'W
{12} 35°04.862'N; 111°41.820'W

Trail length (total), KC East:	2.6 miles
Trail length (total), KC North:	5.5 miles
Trail type:	In-and-out
Challenge level:	Easy to moderate
Elevation change:	550 feet

Llama Trail

Summary: A loop hike with panoramic views of many of Sedona's famous rock formations

Challenge Level: Easy to Moderate

Hiking Distance: About 4.4 miles for the Llama/Bail/Bell Rock Pathway loop; about 6 miles for the Llama/Little Horse/Bell Rock Pathway/Phone Trail loop

Trailhead Directions: From the "Y" roundabout (the intersection of State Route 89A and State Route 179), drive south on SR 179 for about 5 miles to the parking area. After you drive about 3.2 miles, you'll come to the Back O' Beyond roundabout. SR 179 becomes a divided highway just south of the Back O' Beyond roundabout. Continue driving south. About 1.8 miles beyond the Back O' Beyond roundabout, southbound SR 179 adds a passing lane. From the passing lane, turn left at the sign for the "Court House Vista" parking area {1} (it's the second scenic view on the left side of SR 179). You'll see Bell Rock ahead of you on the left side of SR 179. There are toilets at the parking area. The trail starts on the southeast side of the parking area. There is another Llama trailhead off of the Little Horse Trail {8}.

Description: The Llama Trail goes from Bell Rock to the Little Horse Trail. It is a favorite of mountain bicyclists. We prefer to hike it as a loop hike. From the parking area, proceed past the interpretive signboard and follow the Bell Rock Trail 0.1 mile to the intersection with the Bell Rock Pathway {2}. Turn left (northeast) and follow the Bell Rock Pathway 0.3 mile. Continue straight ahead on to the Courthouse Butte Loop Trail {3}. Follow Courthouse Butte Loop for about 300 feet and turn left onto the Llama Trail {4}. In 0.9 mile you'll come to a scenic area with 8 pools of water {5}. Continue another 0.8 mile to the intersection with the Bail Trail {6}. You can turn left here and follow the Bail Trail 0.4 mile to the intersection with the Bell Rock Pathway {7}, or continue 1 mile on the Llama Trail to the Little Horse Trail {8} and turn left to reach the Bell Rock Pathway {9}. Hike south on the Bell Rock Pathway and turn on to the Phone Trail {10} for a shortcut back to the parking area. The Llama Trail approaches Lee Mountain and provides outstanding views of Bell Rock, Courthouse Butte, Twin Buttes and Cathedral Rock. There isn't much shade on this hike so it would be a good choice in cooler weather.

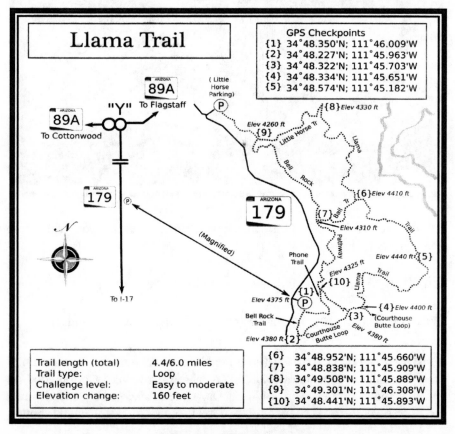

Trail length (total)	4.4/6.0 miles
Trail type:	Loop
Challenge level:	Easy to moderate
Elevation change:	160 feet

GPS Checkpoints
{1} 34°48.350'N; 111°46.009'W
{2} 34°48.227'N; 111°45.963'W
{3} 34°48.322'N; 111°45.703'W
{4} 34°48.334'N; 111°45.651'W
{5} 34°48.574'N; 111°45.182'W

{6} 34°48.952'N; 111°45.660'W
{7} 34°48.838'N; 111°45.909'W
{8} 34°49.508'N; 111°45.889'W
{9} 34°49.301'N; 111°46.308'W
{10} 34°48.441'N; 111°45.893'W

Long Canyon Trail

Summary: An in-and-out hike through a forested canyon with some good red rock views

Challenge Level: Moderate

Hiking Distance: About 3.5 miles each way; 7 miles round trip

Trailhead Directions: From the "Y" roundabout (the intersection of State Route 89A and State Route 179), drive west toward Cottonwood on SR 89A about 3 miles. Turn right on Dry Creek Road (where speed limits are strictly enforced). Stay on Dry Creek Road to a stop sign (about 3

miles) then turn right on Long Canyon Road. Proceed 0.6 mile to the parking area on the left {1}. The trailhead is at the parking area.

Description: This is a nice moderate partially shaded hike through a canyon with red rock views, although some are obstructed. The first 0.75 mile is an old jeep trail. This part of the trail is not shaded and would be very hot in the summer. But once you are in the forest, the trees provide shade. You'll make a sharp left turn after 0.4 mile {2}. You intersect the Deadmans Pass Trail after about 1 mile {3}. You'll see the Seven Canyons golf course on the right. As you continue, the trail becomes more shaded and you cross several washes. We suggest you continue to hike Long Canyon for another 2 miles then begin the return trip {4}.

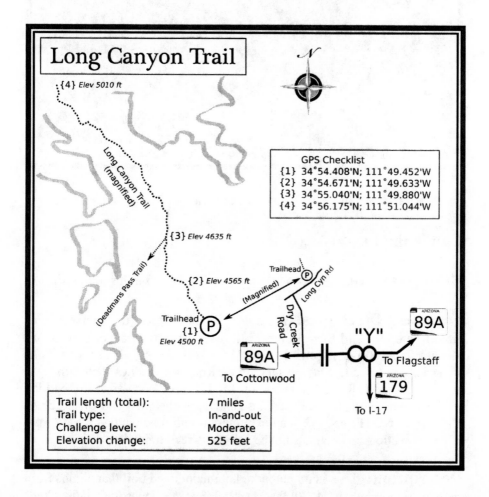

Long Canyon Trail

{4} Elev 5010 ft

Long Canyon Trail (magnified)

GPS Checklist
{1} 34°54.408'N; 111°49.452'W
{2} 34°54.671'N; 111°49.633'W
{3} 34°55.040'N; 111°49.880'W
{4} 34°56.175'N; 111°51.044'W

{3} Elev 4635 ft

Trailhead

(Deadmans Pass Trail)

{2} Elev 4565 ft

(Magnified)

Long Cyn Rd

Trailhead
{1}
Elev 4500 ft

Dry Creek Road

"Y"

ARIZONA
89A

ARIZONA
89A

To Flagstaff

To Cottonwood

ARIZONA
179

To I-17

Trail length (total):	7 miles
Trail type:	In-and-out
Challenge level:	Moderate
Elevation change:	525 feet

Lost Canyon Trail

Summary: An in-and-out hike to an overlook of some Indian ruins

Challenge Level: Moderate

Hiking Distance: About 1.25 mile each way; 2.5 miles round trip

Trailhead Directions: From the "Y" roundabout (the intersection of State Route 89A and State Route 179), drive west toward Cottonwood on SR 89A about 3 miles. Turn right on Dry Creek Road (where speed limits are strictly enforced). Stay on Dry Creek Road for 2 miles then turn right on Forest Road (FR) 152. Proceed on FR 152 for 2.5 miles to the parking area on your right {1}. The parking area is for the west end of the Brins Mesa Trail. NOTE: FR 152 is an extremely rough road beyond the 0.2 mile of paved section so a high clearance vehicle is recommended.

Description: This is an unmarked, unmaintained trail that climbs from an elevation of about 4630 feet to 4980 feet to view some undisturbed

Indian ruins below. Hike the Brins Mesa Trail for some 225 feet (about 75 paces) then turn right to the unmarked Lost Canyon Trail {2}. The red rock views along the trail are very nice. You'll need to watch for improvised cairns to find the trail in places. The trail gradually rises about 80 feet for the first 0.3 mile {3}, then you begin a steep climb of 275 feet to the top of a mesa {4}. As you hike across the mesa for 0.2 mile, the trail comes close to the mesa edge {5}. Continue along the edge of the mesa. There are some impressive red rocks that have fallen from the cliff on your left. To see the ruins below the edge of the mesa, you have to approach the edge of a sheer drop-off; the view is spectacular, but use extreme caution {6}.

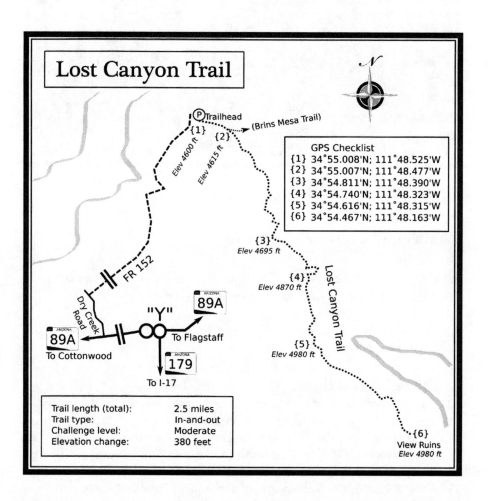

Lost Canyon Trail

P Trailhead
{1}   {2}   (Brins Mesa Trail)

Elev 4600 ft
Elev 4615 ft

GPS Checklist
{1} 34°55.008'N; 111°48.525'W
{2} 34°55.007'N; 111°48.477'W
{3} 34°54.811'N; 111°48.390'W
{4} 34°54.740'N; 111°48.323'W
{5} 34°54.616'N; 111°48.315'W
{6} 34°54.467'N; 111°48.163'W

{3}
Elev 4695 ft

{4}
Elev 4870 ft

Lost Canyon Trail

FR 152

Dry Creek Road

"Y"

ARIZONA 89A

ARIZONA 89A
To Cottonwood

To Flagstaff

ARIZONA 179
To I-17

{5}
Elev 4980 ft

{6}
View Ruins
Elev 4980 ft

Trail length (total):	2.5 miles
Trail type:	In-and-out
Challenge level:	Moderate
Elevation change:	380 feet

Marg's Draw Trail

Summary: An in-and-out hike with great red rock views

Challenge Level: Easy to Moderate

Hiking Distance: About 1.3 miles each way from the Sombart Lane Trailhead to Schnebly Hill Road; 2.6 miles round trip

About 2 miles each way from the Morgan Road Trailhead to Schnebly Hill Road; 4 miles round trip

Trailhead Directions: There are actually three trailheads for this hike: at the south end, at the north end and in the middle of the trail. The south trailhead is at the end of Morgan Road, which is located 1.4 miles south of the "Y" roundabout (the intersection of State Route 89A and State Route 179) on SR 179 {1}. The north trailhead is 1 mile up Schnebly Hill Road, (Schnebly Hill Road is located 0.3 mile south of the "Y" off of SR 179) {4}. The middle trailhead is at the end of Sombart Lane, which is located 0.7 mile south of the "Y" off of SR 179 {2}.

Description: The trail essentially goes north and south, in parallel with SR 179. The south parking area {1} is shared with Broken Arrow and the north parking area {5} is shared with Huckaby and Munds Wagon Trails. You'll encounter a number of "social trails" along the way. For example, about 0.7 mile north of the Broken Arrow trailhead, be sure you take the main trail to the northeast rather than the "social trail" to the west at this intersection {2}. The photo above shows this intersection and the hikers making the correct trail choice. Hiking from the middle trailhead is steep for the first 0.1 mile, then is relatively flat {4}. The hike is close to town so there are residences at either end. But in the middle you are in wilderness and have the feeling of being "away from it all."

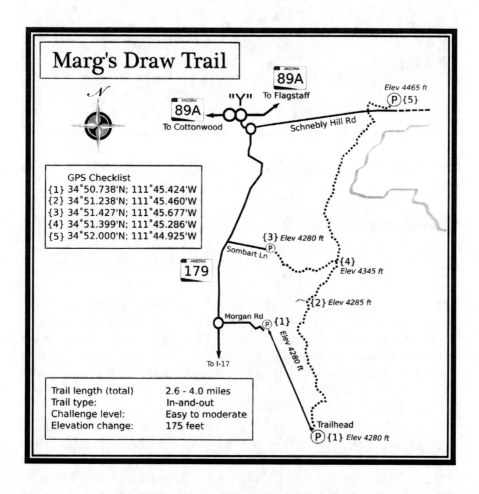

Marg's Draw Trail

GPS Checklist
{1} 34°50.738'N; 111°45.424'W
{2} 34°51.238'N; 111°45.460'W
{3} 34°51.427'N; 111°45.677'W
{4} 34°51.399'N; 111°45.286'W
{5} 34°52.000'N; 111°44.925'W

Trail length (total)	2.6 - 4.0 miles
Trail type:	In-and-out
Challenge level:	Easy to moderate
Elevation change:	175 feet

Mescal Mountain Trail

Summary: An in-and-out trail off the Long Canyon Trail with Indian ruins and panoramic views

Challenge Level: Moderate

Hiking Distance: About 1.3 miles each way; 2.6 miles round trip

Trailhead Directions: From the "Y" roundabout (the intersection of State Route 89A and State Route 179), drive west toward Cottonwood on SR 89A about 3 miles. Turn right on Dry Creek Road (where speed limits are strictly enforced). Follow Dry Creek Road to a stop sign (about 3 miles) then turn right on Long Canyon Road. Proceed 0.6 mile to the parking area on the left {1}. You'll begin by hiking the Long Canyon Trail for 0.6 mile then turn left on the unmarked trail {2}.

Description: This unmarked and unmaintained trail, not found in other guides, gently rises about 100 feet until you reach the intersection with a side trail leading to "Grandma's Cave" on the right after about 0.3 mile {3}. This short, but steep side trip is well worth the effort to get to the "cave," which is more like an overhang. Continuing along the trail to the

90

Mescal Mountain saddle is equally difficult. Near the top you'll climb up to a ledge with a series of shallow caves, where there is evidence of early Indian habitation {4}. Continue left along the ledge where there is an area you will need to scramble up to get to the saddle area. Here there are also early habitation signs and the views are outstanding {5}. While there are steep trails that lead to the top of Mescal Mountain, we prefer to stop at the saddle because the views are outstanding there.

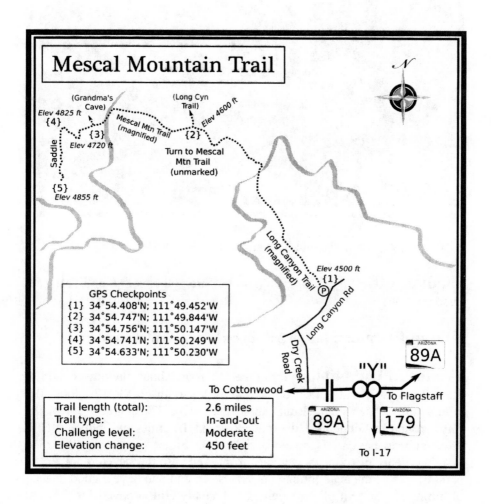

Mitten Ridge Trail

Summary: An in-and-out hike along the base of Mitten Ridge

Challenge Level: Moderate (and be sure you have hiking boots with good traction)

Hiking Distance: About 2 miles each way; 4 miles round trip

Trailhead Directions: From the "Y" roundabout (the intersection of State Route 89A and State Route 179), drive south on SR 179 about 0.3 mile to the Schnebly Hill Roundabout then drive 270 degrees (3/4 of the way) around to Schnebly Hill Road. Proceed 3.7 miles on Schnebly Hill. The trailhead parking is on your right {1}. Either park along the road (leaving plenty of room for vehicles to pass) or use the far entrance to the parking area as the near entrance is very steep and you have a good chance of hitting the bottom of your vehicle. Schnebly Hill is paved for the first mile but the last 2.7 miles can be a very rough unpaved road; a high clearance vehicle is recommended.

Description: You'll be hiking the Cow Pies Trail for the first 0.3 mile. Soon you'll pass by an area dotted with small black rocks, which are pieces of lava. Some believe this to be another powerful vortex area. Sometimes you'll find these rocks placed in the shape of a medicine wheel. Instead of turning left to go to Cow Pies {3}, continue straight ahead to the base of Mitten Ridge. The trail turns left {4}; continue west along the ridge. You'll have to keep your eyes open to follow the trail in some parts. Also, the trail is very narrow with steep drop offs in places. When you arrive at the saddle, which is at the west end of Mitten Ridge, you'll have a nice view of Midgley Bridge and Wilson Mountain to the north {5}.

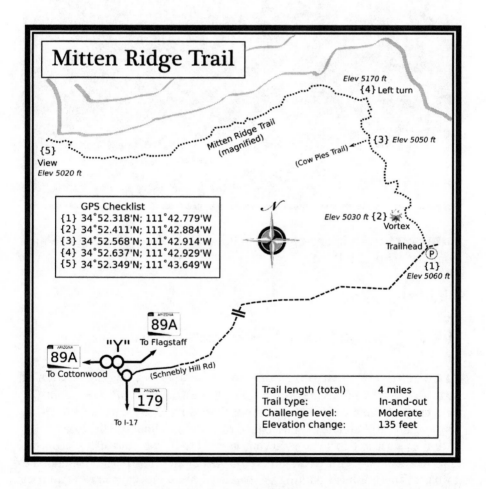

Munds Wagon Trail

Summary: An in-and-out hike following an old road and stream bed along Schnebly Hill Road

Challenge Level: Moderate

Hiking Distance: About 2.5 miles each way; 5 miles round trip

Trailhead Directions: From the "Y" roundabout (the intersection of State Route 89A and State Route 179), drive south on SR 179 about 0.3 mile to the Schnebly Hill Roundabout then drive 270 degrees (3/4 of the way) around to Schnebly Hill Road. Proceed on Schnebly Hill Road for 1 mile then turn left in to the parking area {1}. If you start driving on the unpaved Schnebly Hill Road you've missed the trailhead. Turn around and go back. The trailhead parking is shared with the Huckaby trail. The trail begins on the east side of the parking area. There are toilets at the parking area.

Description: This partially shaded hike follows an old wagon trail along Schnebly Hill Road. You cross Schnebly Hill Road once, then cross back over. If you have a snack with you, there are picnic tables about 1.2 miles along the hike {2}. We have hiked the trail 2.2 miles each way several times {3}. It is much prettier when there is water flowing from snow runoff, which happens in the spring. The trail becomes harder towards the end (about another 1 mile) as you approach a rock formation known locally as "The Carousel" or "Merry-Go-Round."

Munds Wagon Trail

Picnic Tables {2}
Elev 4545 ft

Schnebly Hill Rd

{3}
Elev 4770 ft

Elev 4465 ft
{1}
P

GPS Checklist
{1} 34°52.000'N; 111°44.925'W
{2} 34°52.098'N; 111°44.088'W
{3} 34°52.243'N; 111°43.289'W

(Magnified)

ARIZONA
89A
To Flagstaff

"Y"

ARIZONA
89A
To Cottonwood

P Trailhead

Schnebly Hill Rd

ARIZONA
179

To I-17

Trail length (total)	5 miles
Trail type:	In-and-out
Challenge level:	Moderate
Elevation change:	400 feet

Palatki Heritage Site

Summary: An in-and-out hike to one of the nicest examples of cliff dwellings and rock art of Native Americans in the Sedona area

Challenge Level: Easy

Hiking Distance: About 0.3 mile each way; 0.6 mile round trip to the ruins. Add another 0.3 mile one way, 0.6 mile round trip to the rock art: 1.2 miles total.

Trailhead Directions: From the "Y" roundabout (the intersection of State Route 89A and State Route 179), drive west toward Cottonwood on SR 89A about 3 miles. Turn right on Dry Creek Road (where speed limits are strictly enforced) {1}. Stay on Dry Creek Road to a stop sign (about 3 miles) then turn left on Boynton Canyon Road {2}. Proceed about 1.7 miles to a stop sign. Turn left, continuing on Boynton Pass Road {3}. The first 2 miles are paved, then the road becomes gravel. Drive 4 miles to a stop sign then turn right on Forest Road (FR) 525 {4}. After about 0.1 mile take the right fork, {5} which is FR 795, then continue for another 1.75 miles to the parking area {6}.

Description: Palatki (meaning Red House) is an excellent example of early Native American habitation between about AD 1100 and 1300. It includes cliff dwellings, petroglyphs (etched markings) and pictographs (painted symbols). Because parking is limited at this Heritage Site, you must make a reservation by calling (928) 282-3854; however, there is no cost beyond the cost of a Red Rock Pass (or equivalent). When making a reservation, the ranger will ask your last name, how many in your party and which time slot you want (9:30 am, 11:30 am, or 1:30 pm). After you park, walk to the Visitor Center and check in. Then continue down the path and either go right to the ruins, or left to the rock art. Each trail is about 0.3 mile long. The trail to the cliff dwellings has some rock steps and is steeper than the trail to the rock art. There are rangers and volunteers on duty to give the site's history and answer questions. Pets are not permitted on the site.

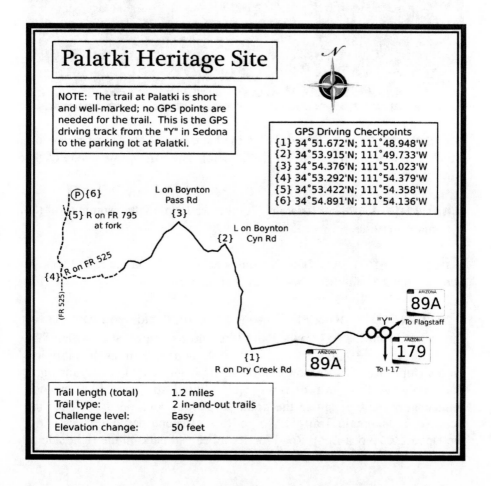

Palatki Heritage Site

NOTE: The trail at Palatki is short and well-marked; no GPS points are needed for the trail. This is the GPS driving track from the "Y" in Sedona to the parking lot at Palatki.

GPS Driving Checkpoints
{1} 34°51.672'N; 111°48.948'W
{2} 34°53.915'N; 111°49.733'W
{3} 34°54.376'N; 111°51.023'W
{4} 34°53.292'N; 111°54.379'W
{5} 34°53.422'N; 111°54.358'W
{6} 34°54.891'N; 111°54.136'W

P {6}

{5} R on FR 795
at fork

L on Boynton
Pass Rd
{3}

L on Boynton
{2}   Cyn Rd

R on FR 525

{4}

(FR 525)

ARIZONA
89A

"Y" To Flagstaff

ARIZONA
179

To I-17

{1}
R on Dry Creek Rd

ARIZONA
89A

Trail length (total)	1.2 miles
Trail type:	2 in-and-out trails
Challenge level:	Easy
Elevation change:	50 feet

Pyramid Trail

Summary: An in-and-out hike up the back side of the "great pyramid," which is visible from the end of the Tabletop Trail off the west side of the Airport Loop Trail.

Challenge Level: Moderate but the trail up to the summit of the pyramid is very steep

Hiking Distance: About 1.5 miles each way; 3 miles round trip: or alternatively 2.5 miles each way; 5 miles round trip

Trailhead Directions: There are two trailheads you can use for this hike. From the "Y" roundabout (the intersection of State Route 89A and State Route 179), drive west on SR 89A about 4.25 miles then turn left on the Upper Red Rock Loop Road. Sedona High School is on your right. Turn right at the third driveway (it's behind the school) then look immediately for the sign to the trailhead parking area on the left for the Schuerman Mountain Trail{1}. To get to the second parking area, follow the Upper Red Rock Loop Road for 1.4 miles and park on the right side of the road {2}. You'll see an unmarked trail heading west on the right.

Description: An unmarked and unmaintained trail you won't find in other guides, there are two ways to hike to the Pyramid. Beginning at the Schuerman Mountain trailhead behind the Sedona High School {1}, hike the Schuerman Mountain Trail for about 500 feet and turn left (south) where the trail forks {3}. Follow this bike path for 1.5 miles to the saddle below the Pyramid {4}. You'll have excellent views of the Pyramid as you hike along. If you begin the hike from the parking area along the road {2}, you'll pass through an opening in a fence after 0.1 mile {5}. Hike westward up to the saddle {4}. The trail is easy to follow but has loose rock and is steep in places. From the saddle {4} hike east up the very steep trail to the top of the Pyramid {6}. From here the view of Cathedral Rock is remarkable. And for the best photos, hike in the afternoon. Backtrack down the Pyramid to the saddle junction, but go straight to follow the trail around to a point with wonderful views of Oak Creek, Mingus Mountain and Red Rock State Park {7}.

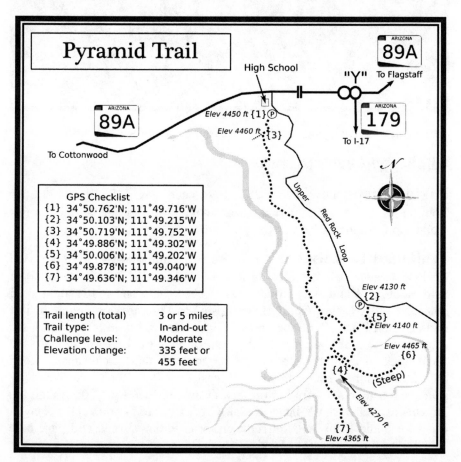

Pyramid Trail

ARIZONA
89A

High School

"Y" To Flagstaff

ARIZONA
89A

Elev 4450 ft {1} Ⓟ
Elev 4460 ft {3}

ARIZONA
179

To I-17

To Cottonwood

Upper Red Rock Loop

N

GPS Checklist
{1} 34°50.762'N; 111°49.716'W
{2} 34°50.103'N; 111°49.215'W
{3} 34°50.719'N; 111°49.752'W
{4} 34°49.886'N; 111°49.302'W
{5} 34°50.006'N; 111°49.202'W
{6} 34°49.878'N; 111°49.040'W
{7} 34°49.636'N; 111°49.346'W

Elev 4130 ft
{2}
Ⓟ
{5}
Elev 4140 ft

Elev 4465 ft
{6}

{4}
(Steep)

Elev 4270 ft

Trail length (total)	3 or 5 miles
Trail type:	In-and-out
Challenge level:	Moderate
Elevation change:	335 feet or 455 feet

{7}
Elev 4365 ft

Rabbit Ears Trail

Summary: An in-and-out hike to a very distinct rock formation

Challenge Level: Moderate

Hiking Distance: About 2.75 miles each way; 5.5 miles round trip from the Bell Rock Vista parking area: about 1.4 miles one way; 2.8 miles round trip from the Jack's Canyon parking area

Trailhead Directions: There are two trailheads for this hike: Bell Rock Vista and on Jack's Canyon Road. From the "Y" (the intersection of State Route 89A and State Route 179) proceed south on SR 179 about 6.25 miles. You'll pass the "Court House Vista" parking area on your left, just north of Bell Rock. Continue on SR 179 another 3/4 mile or so, you'll see another parking area on your left, south of Bell Rock. Turn left into the "Bell Rock Vista" parking area {1}, or (to reach the Jack's Canyon Road trailhead) continue south on SR 179, past the "Bell Rock Vista" parking area about 1 mile and turn left on Jack's Canyon Road (go 270° around the 3rd roundabout in the Village of Oak Creek). Continue on Jack's Canyon Road for about 2 miles. Turn right on to an unpaved road and park here {2}. The trail begins across Jack's Canyon Road.

Description: From the "Bell Rock Vista" parking area, hike northeast for 0.1 mile and turn left on to the Big Park Loop Trail {3}. In 0.4 mile you'll intersect the Courthouse Butte Loop Trail {4}. Turn right. Follow the Loop Trail for 1.2 miles until you descend into a large wash. Look to the right following the Big Park Loop Trail for about 800 feet then turn left and begin climbing up on an unmarked trail that we call the "Ridge Trail" {5}. As you continue east, you'll approach Rabbit Ears. Watch for a faint trail on your left that descends a steep bank when you are southwest of Rabbit Ears if you want a better view {6}{7}.

From the Jack's Canyon Road parking area, walk back on the unpaved road you came in on, turn right when you reach Jack's Canyon and walk about 400 feet to a gate frame on your left. In 0.3 mile, you'll pass through a gate {8}. Continue for another 1 mile and watch for a faint trail on the right to get a better view of Rabbit Ears {6}{7}. There isn't much shade on either of the trails leading to Rabbit Ears so it is a hot hike in the summer. There are very interesting rocks strewn along the trails.

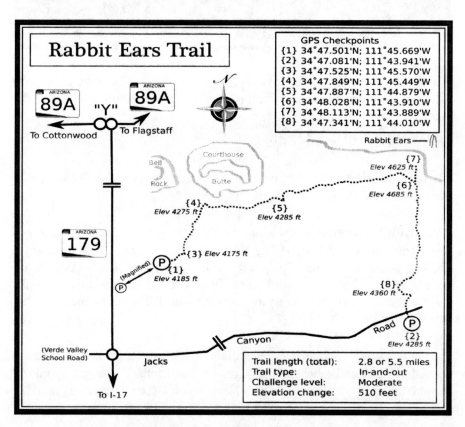

101

Schuerman Mountain Trail

Summary: An in-and-out hike up the side of a mountain with wonderful panoramic views of Cathedral Rock and other notable landmarks

Challenge Level: Moderate

Hiking Distance: About 1 mile to the top, then another 0.25 miles to the southern overlook; 2.5 miles round trip

Trailhead Directions: From the "Y" roundabout (the intersection of State Route 89A and State Route 179), drive west toward Cottonwood on SR 89A about 4.25 miles. Turn left on the Upper Red Rock Loop Road. Sedona High School is on your right. Turn right at the third driveway (it's behind the school) then look immediately for the sign to the trailhead parking area on the left {1}.

Description: Schuerman Mountain Trail provides great views of Cathedral Rock and other red rock views to the south. You begin by hiking behind the Red Rock High School where you'll see a large array of solar panels as big as the school's football field and capable of producing over 800 kilowatts of power (equivalent to powering 125 homes). After 0.2 mile the trail goes around a gate, placed there when cattle once grazed the area. The trail up is steep in places, so watch your footing. If you hike in April, you may encounter wildflowers blooming. When you get to the top {2}, you'll see a "Schuerman Mountain Trail" sign pointing straight ahead (west). We don't recommend hiking this trail because of the many "social trails" that connect to it and the possibility of getting lost. Rather, take the trail to the left (south) for a good view of Cathedral Rock {3}. You can also take the faint (and unmarked) trail to the right to the top to look northwest toward the Verde Valley and Mingus Mountain {4}. Note that the trails on top of Schuerman Mountain are very rocky in places.

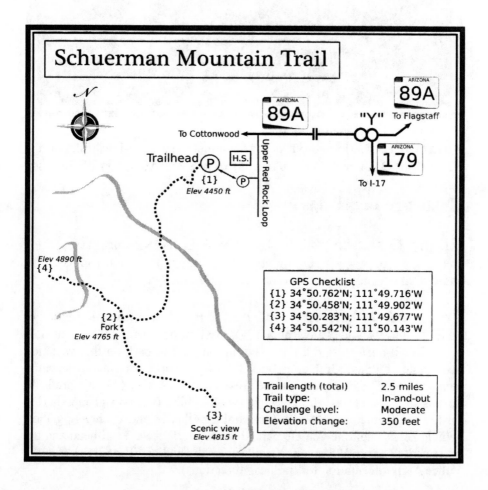

Schuerman Mountain Trail

To Cottonwood

To Flagstaff

"Y"

ARIZONA 89A

ARIZONA 89A

ARIZONA 179

To I-17

Upper Red Rock Loop

Trailhead P H.S.
P
{1}
Elev 4450 ft

Elev 4890 ft
{4}

{2}
Fork
Elev 4765 ft

{3}
Scenic view
Elev 4815 ft

GPS Checklist
{1} 34°50.762'N; 111°49.716'W
{2} 34°50.458'N; 111°49.902'W
{3} 34°50.283'N; 111°49.677'W
{4} 34°50.542'N; 111°50.143'W

Trail length (total)	2.5 miles
Trail type:	In-and-out
Challenge level:	Moderate
Elevation change:	350 feet

Sterling Pass to Vultee Arch Trail

Summary: An in-and-out or a two vehicle "pass-the-key" hike up the west side of Oak Creek Canyon then down to Secret Mountain Wilderness

Challenge Level: Hard

Hiking Distance: About 4.5 miles from the Sterling Pass parking area to the Vultee Arch parking area. About 5.2 miles round trip as an in-and-out hike from Sterling Pass trailhead to Vultee Arch.

Trailhead Directions: From the "Y" roundabout (the intersection of State Route 89A and State Route 179), drive north on SR 89A about 6.25 miles. You'll need to find a wide spot in the road to park on the west side near mile marker 360.4, about 300 feet north of the Manzanita campground. The trail starts on the west side of SR 89A {1}. We prefer to do this hike as a "pass-the-key" two-vehicle hike (i.e. two groups hiking toward each other from the two separate trailheads and exchanging their vehicle keys) with one vehicle parked at the Sterling Pass trailhead and the other parked at the Vultee Arch trailhead at the end of FR 152 {4} (see the Vultee Arch information for trailhead directions).

Description: The parking along SR 89A isn't the best, as there is no official parking area. You'll need to find a wide shoulder on the west side of SR 89A near the trailhead. The trail is steep. There are still many fallen trees from the Brins Fire in 2006. You'll climb about 1150 feet then enter a pine forest. You'll reach the saddle in 1.4 miles then the trail starts down. About 2.4 miles in, you'll come to the sign for Vultee Arch {3}. Hike 0.2 mile down the Vultee Arch Trail to see Vultee Arch, an impressive sight (see Vultee Arch hike description). If you only have one vehicle, retrace your steps back to your vehicle parked along SR 89A.

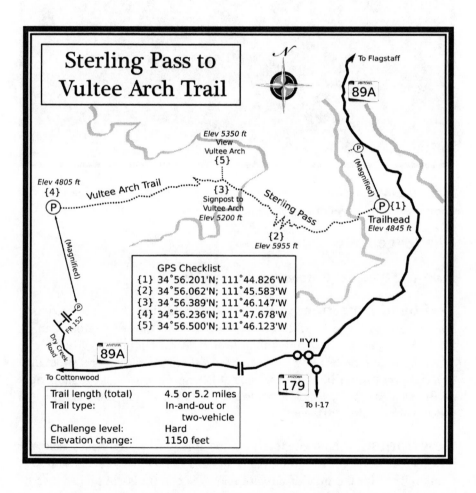

Trail length (total)	4.5 or 5.2 miles
Trail type:	In-and-out or two-vehicle
Challenge level:	Hard
Elevation change:	1150 feet

Sugarloaf Trail

Summary: A short loop hike to a large rock mound with nice views of Capital Butte, Coffeepot and Sedona

Challenge Level: Moderate

Hiking Distance: About 2 miles round trip

Trailhead Directions: From the "Y" roundabout (the intersection of State Route 89A and State Route 179) drive west toward Cottonwood on SR 89A for just under 2 miles then turn right on Coffeepot Drive. Drive about 0.5 mile then turn left on Sanborn. Continue to the second street then turn right on Little Elf. Little Elf ends at Buena Vista so make a short right on Buena Vista then a quick left into the parking area {1}. This is the same parking area as the Coffeepot Trail.

Description: About 50 feet past the interpretive signboard near the parking area, look for a sign on the right {2}. Follow the Teacup/Sugarloaf Summit Trail for 0.3 mile. There are many "social trails" in this area so be sure to follow the cairns. Turn right at the next sign {3} and continue on the Teacup Trail. You'll soon come to a sign for the western end of the Sugarloaf Summit Loop Trail {4}. Rather than turn right here, if you continue straight ahead on the Teacup Trail for another 0.1 mile you'll intersect an unmarked trail on your left that will lead you to the base of Coffeepot Rock {5} (see Coffeepot Trail description). About 0.1 mile further on, turn right on to the Sugarloaf Summit Trail {6} at a sign where you'll have a nice view of Coffeepot Rock. You'll be hiking south, then turn west under a power line. After 0.4 mile you'll see a post on the right, opposite of where the trail to Sugarloaf Summit begins on your left {7}. After climbing to the summit (a scramble of some 0.2 mile that gains 200 feet in elevation) {8}, return to the Sugarloaf Loop Trail and turn left (west). Continue on for another 0.1 mile and turn left on to the Teacup Trail {4} and back to the parking area.

While you'll see rooftops on this in-town hike, the views of Capital Butte (Thunder Mountain) and Coffeepot Rock are beautiful. There is little shade, however, so the hiking would be hot in the summer months.

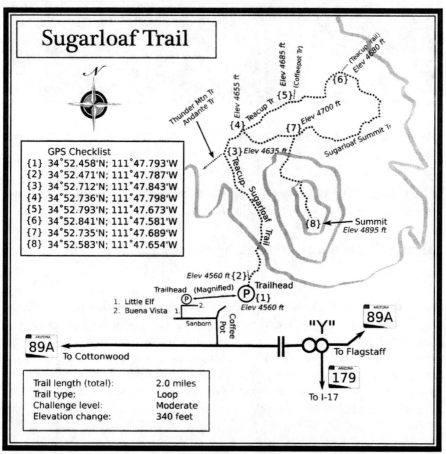

107

Telephone Trail

Summary: A short but steep hike up the east side of Oak Creek Canyon leading to amazing "window" rock formations

Challenge Level: Hard (Note: the trail is very steep in places; do not attempt if the trail is wet or snow is present)

Hiking Distance: About 1.3 miles to the end of the trail; 2.6 miles round trip

Trailhead Directions: From the "Y" (the intersection of State Route 89A and State Route 179), drive north on SR 89A about 10.9 miles to mile post 385.1 and park on the east side of SR 89A on a paved shoulder beneath a 25 foot high cliff. The parking area {1} is 0.4 mile north of the turn to the West Fork parking area. Walk north along SR 89A for 475 feet to the trail sign on your right {2}. The sign is a dark rust color with the corners painted pink (yes pink!).

Description: The trail begins by following along north-bound SR 89A under a telephone line (hence the name of the trail). After 0.3 mile you'll begin a series of steep ascents up to several nice ridges {3}. Along the way there are some very nice rock formations and scenic views of Oak Creek Canyon. At 0.6 mile you'll come to a series of unique "window" or "keyhole" rocks {4}. This would be a good place to have a snack, take some photos and turn back if you don't want to continue on the very steep trail ahead. If you continue on, watch your footing as there are some areas where the trail is very steep with loose pine needles {5}{6}. The trail ends when you reach the top of the east wall of Oak Creek Canyon {7}.

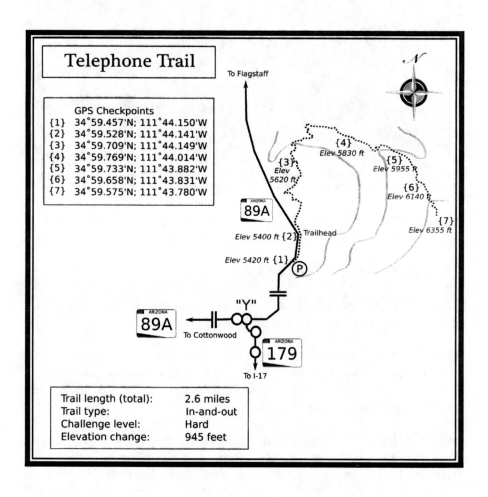

Telephone Trail

GPS Checkpoints
{1} 34°59.457'N; 111°44.150'W
{2} 34°59.528'N; 111°44.141'W
{3} 34°59.709'N; 111°44.149'W
{4} 34°59.769'N; 111°44.014'W
{5} 34°59.733'N; 111°43.882'W
{6} 34°59.658'N; 111°43.831'W
{7} 34°59.575'N; 111°43.780'W

To Flagstaff

{4}
Elev 5830 ft

{3}
Elev
5620 ft

{5}
Elev 5955 ft

{6}
Elev 6140 ft

ARIZONA
89A

Elev 5400 ft {2} Trailhead

{7}
Elev 6355 ft

Elev 5420 ft {1}
P

"Y"

ARIZONA
89A

To Cottonwood

ARIZONA
179

To I-17

Trail length (total):	2.6 miles
Trail type:	In-and-out
Challenge level:	Hard
Elevation change:	945 feet

Templeton Trail

Summary: An in-and-out or a two vehicle "pass-the-key" hike with views of Sedona's major rock formations

Challenge Level: Moderate

Hiking Distance: About 4.2 miles from the Court House Vista parking area to the Baldwin Trail parking area

Trailhead Directions: Park one vehicle at the "Court House Vista" parking area {1} (see Bell Rock Vortex parking directions on page 46) and one vehicle at the Baldwin Trail parking area {7} (see Baldwin Trail parking directions on page 16).

Description: The Templeton Trail extends northwest from the Bell Rock Pathway, just north of Bell Rock and Courthouse Butte to the Baldwin Trail near Oak Creek and Red Rock Crossing. It provides excellent views of Bell Rock, Courthouse Butte, Lee Mountain, Cathedral Rock and many other red rock formations. There are several ways to hike this trail. You can do this hike as a "pass-the-key" two-vehicle hike (i.e. two groups hiking toward each other from the two separate trailheads and exchanging their vehicle keys). If you hike from the "Court House Vista" parking area, look for the Phone Trail on your left about 200 feet past the interpretive signboard {2}. Follow the Phone Trail 0.3 mile and continue north on the Bell Rock Pathway Trail. In 0.1 mile turn left on to the Templeton Trail {3} and follow it beneath both the northbound and southbound lanes of SR 179. You'll have excellent views of Cathedral Rock ahead and in 1 mile you'll intersect the HT Trail on your right {4}. As you approach Cathedral Rock, the landscape becomes high desert. You'll intersect the Cathedral Rock Trail in another 1.3 miles on your right {5} and the short but steep trail to the "saddle" of Cathedral Rock in another 200 feet on your left. As you continue on the Templeton Trail, you'll descend a series of switchbacks and in 0.8 mile you'll be adjacent to Oak Creek, across from "Buddha Beach" and Red Rock Crossing. The Templeton Trail continues on for another 0.2 mile where it intersects the Baldwin Trail {6}. Continue straight ahead on the Baldwin Trail for another 0.5 mile to the Baldwin Trail parking area on Verde Valley School Road {7} for a hike of 4.2 miles.

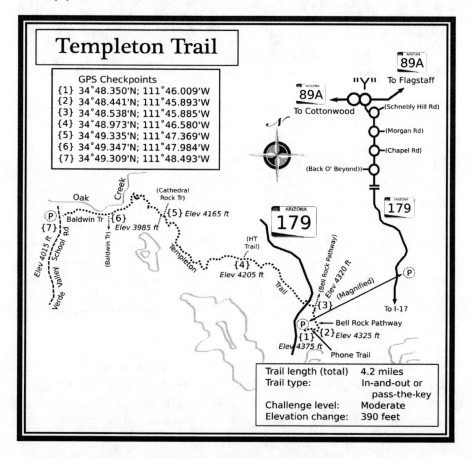

Templeton Trail

	ARIZONA 89A

GPS Checkpoints
{1} 34°48.350'N; 111°46.009'W
{2} 34°48.441'N; 111°45.893'W
{3} 34°48.538'N; 111°45.885'W
{4} 34°48.973'N; 111°46.580'W
{5} 34°49.335'N; 111°47.369'W
{6} 34°49.347'N; 111°47.984'W
{7} 34°49.309'N; 111°48.493'W

ARIZONA 89A

To Cottonwood

"Y" To Flagstaff

(Schnebly Hill Rd)

(Morgan Rd)

(Chapel Rd)

(Back O' Beyond)

N

Oak Creek

(Cathedral Rock Tr)

{5} Elev 4165 ft

ARIZONA 179

P Baldwin Tr {6}
{7} Elev 3985 ft

Elev 4015 ft

Verde Valley School Rd

(Baldwin Tr)

Templeton Trail

(HT Trail)

{4}
Elev 4205 ft

(Bell Rock Pathway)

Elev 4320 ft (Magnified)

P

To I-17

{3}

P Bell Rock Pathway

{1} {2} Elev 4325 ft
Elev 4375 ft
Phone Trail

Trail length (total)	4.2 miles
Trail type:	In-and-out or pass-the-key
Challenge level:	Moderate
Elevation change:	390 feet

Turkey Creek/House Mountain Trail

Summary: A sunny, in-and-out hike through fields, then up steep switchbacks to the summit of House Mountain

Challenge Level: Hard

Hiking Distance: About 3.5 miles each way; 7 miles round trip

Trailhead Directions: From the "Y" roundabout (the intersection of State Route 89A and State Route 179), drive south on SR 179 about 7 miles to the Jack's Canyon and Verde Valley School Road roundabout then turn right (west). Drive approximately 4 miles west on Verde Valley School Road then turn left on to Forest Road 9216B {1}. Drive for about 0.6 mile to the parking area {2}.

Description: From the parking area, hike south on an old road for about 0.3 mile until you reach a fork in the trail {3}. Take the trail to the right to follow the Turkey Creek Trail; the left trail leads to the Twin Pillars. Follow the Turkey Creek Trail for another 1.3 miles and you reach the first of several "tanks" (a man-made depression in the ground that occasionally fills with water) as you approach House Mountain. Along the way, you cross Turkey Creek. Climb up House Mountain for some wonderful views of the red rocks {6}. It's a long steep climb up to the top of House Mountain, but worth the effort.

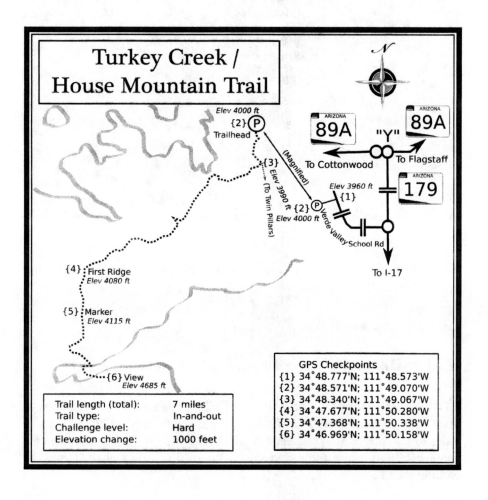

Turkey Creek / House Mountain Trail

Elev 4000 ft
{2} (P) Trailhead

{3} (Magnified)

Elev 3990 ft (To Twin Pillars)

ARIZONA 89A
To Cottonwood

"Y"

ARIZONA 89A
To Flagstaff

Elev 3960 ft
{1}

ARIZONA 179

{2} (P)
Elev 4000 ft

Verde Valley School Rd

To I-17

{4} First Ridge
Elev 4080 ft

{5} Marker
Elev 4115 ft

{6} View
Elev 4685 ft

Trail length (total):	7 miles
Trail type:	In-and-out
Challenge level:	Hard
Elevation change:	1000 feet

GPS Checkpoints
{1} 34°48.777'N; 111°48.573'W
{2} 34°48.571'N; 111°49.070'W
{3} 34°48.340'N; 111°49.067'W
{4} 34°47.677'N; 111°50.280'W
{5} 34°47.368'N; 111°50.338'W
{6} 34°46.969'N; 111°50.158'W

V-Bar-V Petroglyph Site

Summary: A short in-and-out hike to the largest example of petroglyphs in the area

Challenge Level: Easy

Hiking Distance: About 0.5 miles each way; 1 mile round trip

Trailhead Directions: From the "Y" roundabout (the intersection of State Route 89A and State Route 179), drive south on SR 179 about 14.75 miles to the intersection of Interstate 17. Drive under I-17 then continue for another 2.75 miles on the paved Forest Road 618. Turn right {1} into the parking area {2}.

Description: Located south of I-17 off of FR 618, the V-Bar-V Petroglyph Site is a unique experience. There are more than 1000 images created by the Native peoples from about AD 1100 to 1300. It is an easy 0.5 mile hike from the Visitor Center {3} to the rock art site {4} (but the path gets very muddy in wet weather). The views of prehistoric rock art are excellent. Note: the site is normally open Friday through Monday, 9:30 am to 3:30 pm, but you should check with the Sedona Chamber of Commerce Visitor Center or at the Forest Service Ranger Station for days of operation. You do not need a reservation; however, a Red Rock Pass is required to park. Pets are not allowed on the site.

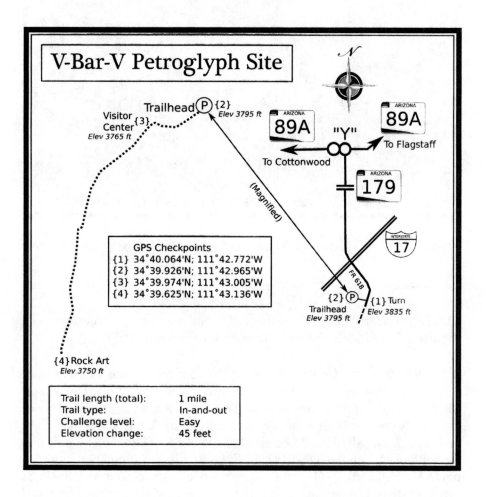

Vultee Arch Trail

Summary: A shady in-and-out hike to a natural red rock arch

Challenge Level: Easy to moderate

Hiking Distance: About 1.9 miles one way to view the arch, add another 0.3 mile to climb up on the arch; 3.8 miles round trip

Trailhead Directions: From the "Y" roundabout (the intersection of State Route 89A and State Route 179), drive west toward Cottonwood on SR 89A about 3 miles. Turn right on Dry Creek Road (where speed limits are strictly enforced). Stay on Dry Creek Road for 2 miles then turn right on Forest Road (FR) 152. Proceed to the end of FR 152 (about 4.5 miles) to the parking area on the left {1}. NOTE: FR 152 is an extremely rough road beyond the 0.2 mile of paved section so a high clearance vehicle is recommended. The parking area is the same as used for the Bear Sign and Dry Creek trails. The Vultee Arch Trail begins on the east side of the parking area, on the right side of the interpretive signboard.

Description: The hike to the arch viewpoint is a relatively easy hike, but it is a scramble (thus the moderate hike rating) to get to the arch so be careful if you attempt this. The trail forks at a signpost {2} after about 1.5 miles; follow the left fork to see the arch. The right fork becomes the Sterling Pass Trail and proceeds to SR 89A in Oak Creek Canyon (see Sterling Pass Trail on page 104). The arch is visible to the north from the view area {3}. Vultee Arch is named after Gerald and Sylvia Vultee who crashed their plane and died nearby in 1938. There is a plaque dedicated to them near the view area for the arch. There are many wildflowers along the trail in late April/early May. Note: the Forest Service reports that the arch is unstable so proceed onto the arch at your own risk.

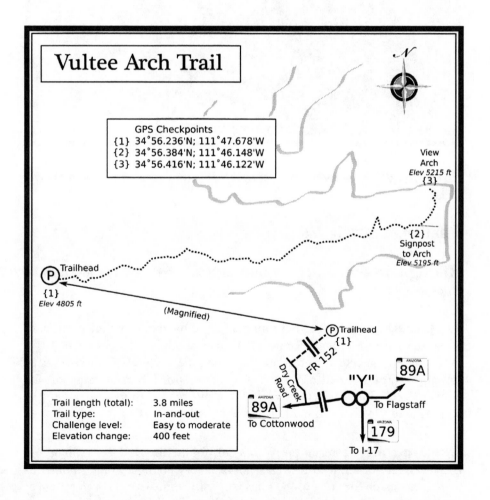

Weir Trail

Summary: A sunny in-and-out trail that follows the path of Wet Beaver Creek

Challenge Level: Moderate

Hiking Distance: About 3 miles each way to the weir (a low dam); 6 miles round trip

Trailhead Directions: From the "Y" roundabout (the intersection of State Route 89A and State Route 179), drive south on SR 179 about 14.75 miles until it intersects Interstate 17. Continue under I-17 then proceed straight on Forest Road 618 for 2 miles then turn left at the sign for the Beaver Creek Ranger Station. Follow the dirt road a short distance to the parking area {1}. There are toilets at the trailhead.

Description: To reach the Weir Trail, follow the Bell Trail along Wet Beaver Creek for a few miles. This can be a very hot hike in the summer as there is no shade for most of the hike. You will come across several trails as you hike along. The first one is the White Mesa Trail at about 1.75 miles

{2}. The next trail you come across is the Apache Maid Trail at 2.25 miles {3}. You'll intersect the short Weir Trail in another 0.2 mile, which goes down to the creek. While the rock-strewn Bell Trail {4} goes on, a good stopping place is at the weir in the shade {5}.

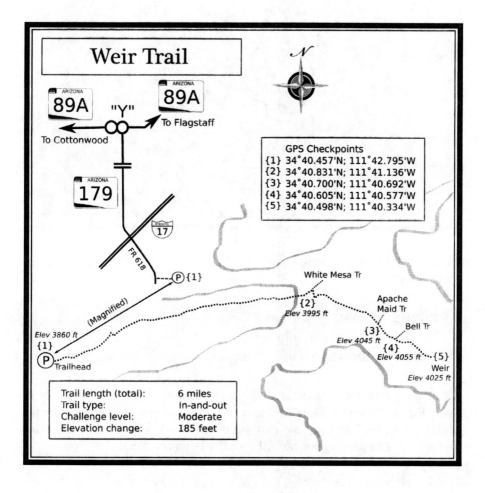

Wilson Canyon Trail

Summary: A pleasant in-and-out hike in a shaded canyon with red rock views

Challenge Level: Moderate

Hiking Distance: About 1.5 miles each way; 3 miles round trip

Trailhead Directions: From the "Y" roundabout (the intersection of State Route 89A and State Route 179), drive north on SR 89A to the Midgley Bridge. The trailhead parking is on your left just as you cross the bridge {1}. The parking lot can fill up quickly on the weekends.

Description: The trailhead is away from SR 89A at the far end of the parking area, just beyond the picnic table pavilion. You'll quickly come to the Wilson Mountain Trail {2}. Continue straight ahead. At first, the trail is wide but narrows further on. At about 0.5 mile, you'll intersect the end of the Jim Thompson Trail {3}. The Wilson Canyon trail crosses the bottom of the canyon about a dozen times as it winds in about 1.6 miles. You'll be hiking among scrub oak and small Arizona Cypress. The trail becomes somewhat narrow about 1 mile in. After 1.3 miles you'll come to a sign marking the end of the trail. Stop here or continue up the wash for another 75 feet and watch for a steep side trail on your right {4}. Scramble up unto the nearby rock outcropping for some terrific views all around. If you continue on even farther up the wash, you begin hiking uphill and the views become much better {5}.

Wilson Canyon Trail

{5} Elev 4950 ft

GPS Checkpoints
{1} 34°54.023'N; 111°44.901'W
{2} 34°53.162'N; 111°44.499'W
{3} 34°53.551'N; 111°44.507'W
{4} 34°53.961'N; 111°44.880'W
{5} 34°54.022'N; 111°44.891'W

(Side trail)

{4}
Elev 4830 ft

Intersect Jim
Thompson Trail {3}
Elev 4590 ft

Intersect Wilson
Mtn South Trail {2}
Elev 4540 ft

To Flagstaff P

Trailhead
P {1}
Elev 4530 ft

"Y"
ARIZONA
89A

ARIZONA
89A

ARIZONA
89A
To Cottonwood

Midgley Bridge

ARIZONA
179
To I-17

Trail length (total):	3 miles
Trail type:	In-and-out
Challenge level:	Moderate
Elevation change:	420 feet

Wilson Mountain South Trail

Summary: A sunny in-and-out hike to the top of Wilson Mountain, the highest mountain in the Sedona area.

Challenge Level: Hard

Hiking Distance: About 5 miles each way to the top; 10 miles round trip

Trailhead Directions: From the "Y" roundabout (the intersection of State Route 89A and State Route 179), drive north on SR 89A to the Midgley Bridge. The trailhead parking is on your left just as you cross the bridge {1}. The parking lot can fill up quickly on the weekends.

Description: From the Midgley Bridge parking area, you'll hike up switchbacks for 2.4 miles with a 1600 foot elevation change to the "first bench," a long plateau running the length of the east side of the mountain {3}. From there, you go another mile and 800 feet higher to the tool shed where fire tools are stored. From there, you turn left (south) to a high point (7000+ feet, the highest mountain in Sedona). At the top, you can see the

San Francisco Peaks to the north in Flagstaff. Go another 0.25 mile to the edge for fantastic views overlooking Sedona {4}. Because of the elevation, the trail may be snow-covered in the winter and we do not recommend hiking this trail at that time.

Wilson Mountain South Trail

{4} Summit
Elev 6975 ft

Reach First Bench {3}
Elev 6175 ft

GPS Checkpoints
{1} 34°54.023'N; 111°44.901'W
{2} 34°53.651'N; 111°44.537'W
{3} 34°54.480'N; 111°44.414'W
{4} 34°55.304'N; 111°45.500'W

Right turn {2}
Elev 4700 ft

To Flagstaff (P)

"Y"

89A

89A

To Cottonwood

179

To I-17

Midgley Brudge

(Magnified)

Elev 4530 ft

(P) {1}

Trail length (total):	10 miles
Trail type:	In-and-out
Challenge level:	Hard
Elevation change:	2400 feet

Woods Canyon Trail

Summary: A sunny in-and-out hike along Dry Beaver Creek

Challenge Level: Moderate

Hiking Distance: About 2.5 miles each way; 5 miles round trip

Trailhead Directions: From the "Y" roundabout (the intersection of State Route 89A and State Route 179), drive south on SR 179 about 8.75 miles then turn in to the Red Rock Ranger Station {1}. Follow the drive then turn right at the first road rather than following the road to the left to the Visitor Center. The trailhead is at the far south end of the parking area {2}.

Description: Just after you begin the trail, you will cross a small ditch, which always seems to have water in it. You'll shortly come to a gate {3}. The trail proceeds up a canyon and follows the path of Dry Beaver Creek.

You'll come to a sign-in box after 1 mile {4}. After about 2 miles, you'll pass through a second gate {5} and soon intersect the Hot Loop Trail {6}. Continue straight on Woods Canyon Trail for another 0.3 mile and make a right turn to go down to Dry Beaver Creek {7}. Here you'll see large river rocks, which are deposited when Dry Beaver Creek floods {8}. The Creek usually flows in the springtime because of the snow melt to the north. We usually stop there, but the trail continues on for another 2.5 miles, becoming more difficult the further you go. Wildflowers are in abundance in April most years. There is little shade on this hike so it will be hot in the summer.

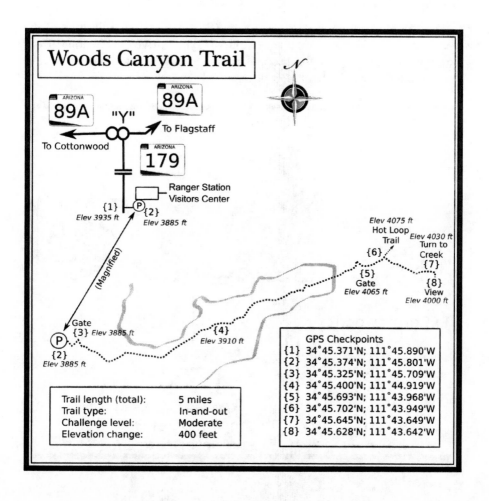

Definition of the "Y"

If you obtain directions from a Sedona local, chances are he or she will give you those directions referencing something called the "Y." We use the "Y" as our reference point in this guidebook also. Some history is in order.

Before the age of roundabouts (traffic circles), there was a traffic light at the intersection of State Route 89A and State Route 179. If you could look at that intersection with a bird's eye view, it would have looked like an elongated letter "Y." And that is why locals refer to that intersection as "the Y."

The traffic light at the intersection of State Routes 89A and 179 has been replaced by two roundabouts so the intersection is really no longer in the shape of a "Y" but the reference continues. So, if you come to Sedona by driving north on SR 179, the "Y" is the northern end of SR 179.

If you drive to Sedona from Flagstaff on SR 89A, the "Y" is the first of the two roundabouts you come to. And, if you drive to Sedona from Cottonwood, the "Y" is the second roundabout you enter, which is very close to the first roundabout.

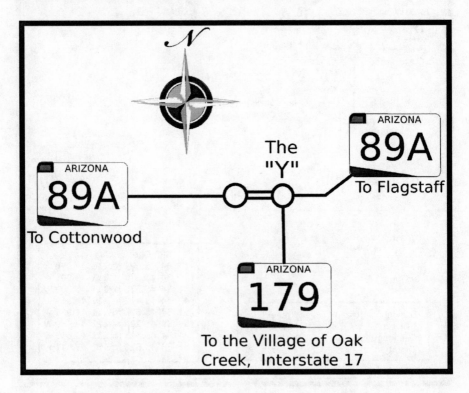

Scenic Drives

Here are several scenic drives around the Sedona area where you can take some excellent photographs of the red rock formations. All of the roads mentioned below are paved, with the exception of Schnebly Hill Road, which is paved only for the first mile. The "Y" roundabout referenced below is the intersection of State Route 89A and State Route 179.

Airport Overlook

Atop Airport Mesa is a scenic overlook, which provides magnificent views of Coffeepot Rock, Thunder Mountain, Sugarloaf and Chimney Rock. Looking west across the Verde Valley, you'll see the Black Hills; on a clear day you can even see the "J" above Jerome, Arizona.

From the "Y" roundabout, drive west toward Cottonwood on SR 89A for 1 mile and turn left on Airport Road. Proceed up Airport Road for 1.1 miles to the scenic overlook on your right. The free parking area is on your left at GPS coordinates: 34° 51.178' N; 111° 47.390' W. Once you have parked, cross the road and enjoy the view. Donations are accepted to help maintain the overlook.

Sedona's Namesake (Sedona Schnebly)

The grave of Sedona Schnebly, for whom the town is named is located off Airport Road. Drive up Airport Road a short distance and turn right at the Elk's Club sign, just beyond the U Haul trailer rental facility. Park in front of the "Cook's Cedar Glade Cemetery" arch on your right and proceed north about 75 paces to GPS coordinates 34° 51.685' N; 111° 46.866' W. Inside the low wall you'll find the grave of Sedona Schnebly (1877-1950).

Bell Rock/Courthouse Butte/Lee Mountain

Bell Rock is one of the most recognizable rock formations in Sedona. And Courthouse Butte, along with Lee Mountain, are sights many visitors first see when they arrive in Sedona driving north on State Route 179. There are two parking areas at Bell Rock, one to the north named the Court House Vista and one to the south named the Bell Rock Vista. You can take photographs of Bell Rock, Courthouse Butte and Lee Mountain any time of day because from the Bell Rock Vista, the sun will be behind you.

From the "Y" roundabout, travel south on State Route 179 about 7 miles. First you'll see the Courthouse Vista parking area on your left. Proceed on SR 179 for another 1 mile then turn into the Bell Rock Vista parking area. From here you'll have great views of the rock formations.

Chapel of the Holy Cross

This isn't a scenic drive in the true sense, but the Chapel of the Holy Cross is a local landmark and a must see. It was opened in 1956 and serves as a place to meditate and enjoy the beauty that is Sedona.

From the "Y" roundabout, proceed south on SR 179 about 2.8 miles then drive 270 degrees (3/4 of the way) around the Chapel Road roundabout. Proceed east on Chapel Road to the end. The Chapel has a gift shop located in the lower level.

Take time to observe the fine views from the Chapel. There is no charge to park or enter the Chapel, but donations are accepted.

Oak Creek Canyon
The drive up Oak Creek Canyon is a world-famous route that always delights. You begin in Sedona and drive toward Flagstaff to the Scenic View Area. As you follow along the path cut by Oak Creek over millions of years, the views and solitude are beautiful. Cell phone use is limited in Oak Creek Canyon. You'll go up in elevation from about 4500 feet (Sedona) to 6400 feet (at the Scenic View Area).

From the "Y" roundabout, proceed north on SR 89A through Uptown Sedona. As you proceed, you'll probably want to pull over and take photographs. Be sure you pull off the road far enough to let vehicles pass by. Drive up Oak Creek Canyon for 16 miles and turn right into the Scenic View Area. If you did the driving up Oak Creek Canyon, ask someone else to drive back to Sedona so you can enjoy the views.

Schnebly Hill Road
We suggest you have a high-clearance vehicle for this drive. Schnebly Hill Road is paved for the first 1 mile and the views don't begin until the very rough unpaved portion of the road. In wet weather, the gate at the end of the pavement is sometimes closed because of road conditions. Also, in winter Schnebly Hill Road is closed about 4.3 miles in at the "Merry-Go-Round." If the gate is open, proceed on for another 1.7 miles to the Schnebly Hill Vista at GPS coordinates: 34° 53.385' N; 111° 42.194' W for some amazing views. If you stop along the road, be sure to pull your vehicle far enough off the road to let other vehicles by.

From the "Y" roundabout, go south on SR 179 about 0.3 mile to the Schnebly Hill Roundabout then drive 270 degrees (3/4 of the way) around to Schnebly Hill Road. Proceed 1 mile on paved road then continue on the unpaved section of Schnebly Hill Road. If the road is not closed, you can drive all the way to Interstate 17, but after about 6 miles, there are minimal views.

Upper Red Rock Loop Road
The drive on the Upper Red Rock Loop Road provides outstanding views of Cathedral Rock, with Courthouse Butte and Bell Rock in the distance. It is the road to Crescent Moon Ranch/Red Rock Crossing, where you can stroll along the banks of Oak Creek and take photographs of Cathedral Rock with Oak Creek in the foreground, one of the most recognized photographic settings in Sedona. Be sure to go there in the afternoon as you'll be looking to the east where the sun rises. A late afternoon photo will be one you'll cherish.

From the "Y" roundabout, drive west on SR 89A about 4.25 miles then turn left on the Upper Red Rock Loop Road. Follow the Upper Red Rock Loop Road for about 1.9 miles for the best views. If you want to continue to Crescent Moon Ranch/Red Rock Crossing, turn left on Chavez Ranch Road then follow it about 1 mile to the end until you reach the entrance gate.

Index

Index

CPSIA information can be obtained at www.ICGtesting.com
Printed in the USA
LVOW12s0245211013

357826LV00001B/91/P

9 781466 429154